Does My Work Matter?

The Hidden Treasure in the Work We Do

by C. R. Baugh, Ph.D.

With True Accounts From the Lives of

Darvin Avis	Michael Fargo	Jerry Minifie
Gwen Barrett	John Gilman	Serena Morones
Ben Benjamin	Charlie Glendinning	Dick Sawdey
Katy Crane	Kent Hotaling	Bill Simmons
Michelle DeYoung	Jay Jayapalan	Lyn Swanson
Dianne Doherty		Mark Thomas

Cover Designed by: Jay Jayapalan

Published October, 2011 by C. R. Baugh and Associates
Seattle, WA 98199

ISBN-13: 978-1466320277
ISBN-10: 1466320273

Dedication

During the publishing of this book, John Gilman unexpectedly discovered he had brain cancer and died shortly thereafter. This book is dedicated to him as his long-standing interest in this topic was a major stimulus for the creation of this work.

Endorsements

"Rick Baugh's storytellers do more than describe their career successes and failures. They tell us of their discovery of the real value of work and how they have come to cope with and conquer the challenges that face us all. Not one story dwells on material success, but they all celebrate those rich moments when people discover real purpose in their lives. Eavesdropping on their life journeys can help you draw your own map."
> **The Honorable Dick Durbin, U. S. Senator from Illinois, Springfield, IL**

"We all work, but few of us get beyond the prevailing sense that work is about rewards, compromises and endurance. Rick Baugh and his colleagues give us a perspective that is both inspiring and helpful - a way to recognize the significance of what we do and allow that recognition to liberate us."
> **Dr. Lee Huntsman, Ph.D., Former President, University of Washington, Seattle, WA**

"In a world where the majority of people say that they would like to find a new job, Rick Baugh offers his readers practical insights and perspectives on how to think differently about work. He takes us on a series of journeys that remind us first and foremost that people are special and important, and that everyone can find meaning, purpose and significance in their work."
> **Mr. Michael A. Volkema, Chairman of the Board, Herman Miller, Inc., Zeeland, MI**

"Rick Baugh exposes the truth that you can have a work life that is both rewarding and fulfilling. What is even more interesting is that this can be attained in many different ways and in many different career choices. The common threads he brings out ring true. Caring about others, servicing others can be fulfilling and bring value to life and a career."
> **Mr. Don Hendler, President and CEO, Leviton Manufacturing Company, Melville, NY**

"Author Rick Baugh, in the true stories he features, has masterfully illustrated one very simple principle, that is the adoption of a people-oriented attitude will help us, or in some cases an organization, to succeed. This attitude can also enrich the contributions we make and turn our career into a meaningful and rewarding one."

Dr. Nim Cheng, Ph.D.,
Former President of the Communications Society of The Institute for Electrical and Electronics Engineers, New York, NY,
CEO, Hong Kong Applied Science and Research Technology Institute (ASRTI), People's Republic of China

"Whether you are starting a career or are an experienced member of the workforce . . . all of us want to know whether our work really matters. Author Rick Baugh through stories of everyday folks, provides not only a clear answer to the question, but how all of us can make a difference in the communities we serve. A nice tapestry of things we know, woven with people that live next door to us."

Mr. Doug Stewart, Former President and CEO, Insurance Company

"Our work is important; it defines who we are. It does not matter whether you are a teacher, an assembly-line worker, a homemaker or a special operator. Reaching your potential in your chosen field empowers yourself and inspires those around you."

Mr. Dick Couch, Author of *The Warrior Elite* and *Chosen Soldier*, U. S. Navy SEAL, Retired, Sun Valley, ID

"One of the great losses in our day has been the loss of understanding that all work matters. This writing helps the idea of "vocation" come to life and illustrates the great creativity with which many have worked it out in faithful and unique ways!"

Dr. Steve Moore, Ph.D., Executive Director, Murdock Trust, Vancouver, WA

Readers' Comments

"In an economic landscape where a straight career path is no longer possible, Baugh provides nourishment for the sometimes long and lonely journey. As a full-time mom who desires to integrate career goals with raising a family, these unique and personal stories demonstrate that it's not only possible, but desirable, to discover a direction that will meaningfully employ my own unique gifts and abilities. Baugh gives me hope that the route with the most curves and rest stops may also be the most fulfilling."

Mrs. Susan Fikse, Full-time Mother and Freelance Writer, Atlanta, GA

"So often the people in management positions are unaware of leadership skills. If employees and managers learn to embrace the principals of the three C's (competency, character and caring) it will enhance the effectiveness of each person involved in the business environment. This book advocates the prioritizing of individual development as an investment towards achieving the vision of the business. Rick points the way to creating an environment where individual motives support the work-force and business, rather than sabotaging management goals and individuals for personal gain which unfortunately is often the norm. This book works to change that."

Mr. Jeff Nixon, Sergeant, Municipal Police Force, NJ

"What a refreshing perspective on career and personal worth. The book helps you re-frame the "what" you do on a daily basis and, if you allow it, challenges the "why" you do it as well. Just a great heart-check."

Mr. Craig Cook, Sales Representative, Major Pharmaceutical Manufacturer, Pasadena, CA

"Research indicates that finding meaning and purpose in our work is vital for our well-being. Rick Baugh is a gifted guide whose sage advice in *Does My Work Matter?* helps to navigate this journey of self-discovery,"

Dr. Baldwin Way, Ph.D., Assistant Professor, Department of Psychology and Institute for Behavioral Medicine, The Ohio State University, Columbus, OH

"I have not only experienced the true satisfaction associated with building strong client relationships through the 3 C's approach, but I also encourage my team to embrace these concepts. Rick Baugh's use of real life anecdotes in *Does My Work Matter* provides excellent insight into understanding the true value of one's work in the context of both self-discovery and career development. I now look at professional challenges as part of my individual path, which helps me understand the real value of my work."

Ms. Kelly Bullington, Sales Manager, Google Inc., Mountain View, CA

Does My Work Matter?
The Hidden Treasure in the Work We Do

Table of Contents

Introduction: The Hidden Treasure in the Work I Do

As I drive up to the AT&T Bell Laboratories building on the first day of my first real job, I am filled with anticipation. After spending twenty years in school, I am eager to get fully engaged in science and engineering on "real" problems that bring innovative products to market. But a few short months later, my enthusiasm has mostly drained as I see too many of my "taskmaster" cohorts getting promotions. Since management declares values by who gets promotions, the executives honor and reward whip cracking people who get the job done at the expense of making the work fun for people, inspiring individuals to great accomplishments, or even caring about the well-being of employees. By implication, employees are used to get tasks completed and their concerns are valid only if they help get the work done. (Of course, not all people receiving promotions are "whip crackers" but, I conclude, too many are.)

I do not want to become one of these relentless taskmasters who get rewards for their essentially selfish behavior – building their career on the backs of those doing most of the work. I do not want to be like that, I do not like success being defined like that. And I surely do not want my daughter marrying someone like that. My restlessness and uneasiness grows as my observations mushroom into a full blown dilemma. It dawns on me that I have no alternative approach. Would I have to become like them to be fully engaged or did an alternative exist? I realize I have no answer to the question of what purpose drives my work. What is going to propel my motivation for the next 40 years of my career? Is my aspiration for having a career that contributed to society in a way that leads to a deep sense of satisfaction going to be dashed on the rocks of reality?

I am beset by the question: "Does my work matter?" Will all of my hard work, creative energy, endurance of drudgery, daily commitments, and exhausting efforts working alongside difficult people ever lead to anything worthwhile? Why am I doing all this? Am I doomed to a career of purposelessness? Is work going to suck the life out of me? And I notice some of my contemporaries are also asking themselves the same profound questions. Thus begins an exciting adventure, although it did

1

not feel like that many a time! My colleagues and I are on a quest to find a reason that would result in a deeply engrained motivation for inspiring an entire career in the highly dynamic world of telecommunications.

In those early years, I did not know I was missing the right vantage point for viewing my work. I was not looking in the right places nor was I asking the right questions to find my purpose for my work. The lack of a realistic place from which to "see" my career led me to the default position of comparing myself to others. As a result, I was not free to ignore these flawed views of a successful career and simply concentrate on discovering my own unique purpose for why the work I did mattered. But after a long period of discovery with paths pursued that ended in dead ends, with fits-and-starts, and misguided goals chased, I eventually encountered the proverbial light at the end of the tunnel. Eventually I saw work in a totally new context from a totally different vantage point, dramatically changing my journey.

That's why I have written this book. By reading about my journey and the journeys of many others, the hope is that you will be able to discover an invigorating and motivating purpose for the unique reason you do the work you do. The right vantage point will save you both wasted time and effort because you will have more confidence and less doubt that you are on the right path. And since many readers may well be on the right path (even if they do not know it), the principles explained and the stories shared will affirm and encourage your journey.

Probably most of you grew up like me – not knowing that a career could be filled with significance. My dad was an industrial chemist who never gave me a clue as to whether he hated or loved his job. As far as I could tell, it was just something he did, like putting out the garbage each week. Work served the purpose of providing an income for the family. My mom worked part-time because she enjoyed the collegiality of her boss and co-workers. As far as I could tell, she worked because it was a nice way to fill her time and was a necessary addition to the family income. Neither parent seemed to have a higher purpose for working.

My parent's friends did not seem to view their jobs any differently. They did not light up when talking about the office or factory the way they beamed when talking about golf, gardening or woodworking. I cannot recall a single conversation with my parents or their friends in which they assured me that my career could be a fantastic experience. The advice that I do remember was to find a career that would make me rich very quickly so I could quit working and move on to something enjoyable. *The hidden message:* Work is something you have to do but would not choose to do if you didn't need the money. Look elsewhere if you want to add meaning and purpose to your life.

Growing up I heard adults talk about their eagerness to retire and get away from the daily torture of their pointless job or a demeaning boss. Older adults talked about the day they retired as the best day of their life. It even topped the day they got married. Their disdain for their job had that degree of intensity. *The hidden message*: Work has no higher purpose or connection with making society better. Look elsewhere if you want to impact society in any major way.

As I formulated my outlook on work, I was bombarded by news stories of deceptive businesspeople who defrauded people or underhanded businessmen who exploited workers or customers. *The hidden message*: Business is an ugly endeavor filled with evil people who prey upon the unsuspecting. Look elsewhere if you want to be involved in highly respected activities with honorable people.

I was never encouraged to find out what was important to do or what was of interest to me and then find a way to get paid to do it. I had no idea that work could be a place of:

- Invigorating meaning and purpose
- Being part of something exciting and worthwhile
- Making a difference in people's lives
- Making society better through the creation of products and services that benefit people
- Contributing to solving world problems as significant as poverty or hunger

I concluded that work was something to endure. I had no understanding of how my profession could be a major source of significance in my life or a place to find importance in the products and services I produced.

My conclusion was wrong!

Contrary to all the messages I heard growing up, our careers, jobs, professions or avocations can be filled with lasting significance. And when I entered the workforce myself, I began to see the hopelessness of my outlook on work. I desired a different perspective, and you will read

3

about my search in the coming pages. Ultimately, I learned that I can have a career that has the kind of meaning that George Bernard Shaw described in his play *Man and Superman*[1]:

> *This is the **true joy in life**, . . . the being a force of Nature . . . the only real tragedy in life is to be used by personally minded men for purposes you recognize as base.*

I too want my work to leave a legacy and to be a "force of Nature" for something good that generates a sense that what we do has significance because of its contribution to society.

What the Book is

The fact that so few people I knew found work to be this rewarding does not prove that work has little meaning. Rather, it suggested that the truth was hidden and I had to search for it. This manuscript centers on helping you find your hidden treasure of incredible meaning and purpose in your job – because your work does matter. It requires us to find the *vantage point* for viewing our work. The *right framework or context* allows us to finally "see" the *meaningful purpose* in the work we do.

The book expands on two major themes:

1. I describe the vantage point in detail, show its applicability to our work environments, and provide evidence that it is comprehensive enough to meet the challenges of our work place. I also illustrate how people from many different walks of life navigated this transformative journey of discovery. My desire is that it convinces you to stay the course until you, too, uncover the hidden treasure in the work you do.

2. I elaborate on a few principles that naturally derive from adopting this vantage point. The discussion of the details proves that the proposed context for viewing work serves us well, matches up with the realities of the work place, and leads to successful organizations and effective individuals. In other words, the vantage point can be trusted, especially during those times when we have serious doubts that the

---

[1]George Bernard Shaw, *Man and Superman: a Comedy and a Philosophy,"* (Brentano's, NYC, 1916, Play, copyright 1903), Epistle Dedicatory to Arthur Bingham Walkley, pp. xxxi-xxxii (emphasis in excerpt is added).

path we are on will lead us to our unique purpose for the work we do.

This book presents both principles and illustrative stories from ordinary people who live and work in ordinary careers. They persisted in their vocations until they found the hidden treasure of purpose that brought a deep sense of passion to their daily work lives. Some did have the good fortune to be in the right place at the right time and saw their contributions propel them to unexpected places. Some have a faith foundation for their lives, and their stories naturally include that component. Others found purpose apart from spiritual belief.

In the last few years, I have had the pleasure of having a front-row seat as dozens of people systematically uncover the hidden meaning of their work. By taking advantage of a carefully crafted innovation and incubation environment, I help them invent their unique careers – sort through the confusion they have over their career path, overcome barriers to action, and take proactive steps that gave clarity and direction. Some of the wisdom I have gleaned as I have watched them discover meaning in their journeys has found its way into this book.

I am aware that there are many people who have had success in their careers using a very different vantage point than the one I am describing. However, the framework I explain in detail is worthy of consideration and takes into consideration the realities we face in our careers and avocations. It does result in a deeply satisfying career as all the people depict in their stories. Moreover, it is very synergistic with marriage, parenting, and friendship.

Let's Get Going

Having the right vantage point for looking at our work becomes an incredible asset for uncovering the hidden treasure. A first step of the discovery process is a framework that "sees" the nobility of work and how to reorient our thinking to see its real importance to society. When we finally know why we esteem our work as important, we not only have a motivating purpose for working but we also are invigorated by the specific work we do.

We also will look at a few principles associated with the vantage point and give examples of successful businesses and individuals who incorporated these principles – including specific examples of a principle not often considered a component of work: love. We'll discuss the tools that all workers will want to develop in order to both carry out their purpose and be effective in their careers.

My desire is that you might find parts of your unfolding story somewhere in these ideas and stories, that they put words to what you have experienced, are experiencing and will experience. I hope you will be able to relax with your uncertainties about the future and gain confidence that your path will lead to finding the hidden treasure in your work – a deep sense of purpose and meaning that fuels a passion for what you do.

The Vantage Point for Discovery – Section I

Finding Meaning and Purpose for Work

When I finished graduate school in computer science in 1970 and joined AT&T Bell Laboratories as a member of the telecommunications research staff, I was surprised by the hard question that began to gnaw at me. Up until that point I had been working furiously on the prerequisites to work. Once I finished them, I moved to the starting line of my career, stepped into the blocks and heard the gun sound. I was off to the races – or had I just entered the rat race?

A question I had never considered nipped at my heels, and I just couldn't shake it: What is the point of all this work? Why would I commit so much of my life to something that competes with my marriage, family and friends? Surely the answer involved a purpose greater than keeping my stomach full.

As the digital age loomed, I didn't have much time to stop and really consider the question. I was too busy at work trying to learn a new job that itself was constantly changing. It took me several years to slow down, step back and begin to gain a broader vantage point from which to see why my work matters. Once I did, instead of finding answers, I was faced with more questions. Two of them emerged as crucial for discovering why my work matters:

1. Why is my industry important to society?
2. Why is my role critical even though I am totally replaceable?

I wasn't interested in answers that merely acknowledged facts or that I merely professed; but ones I truly believed, ones – as Dallas Willard, professor of philosophy at the University of Southern California, says – for which "my whole being is set to act as if something was so."[2] I desired an answer to which I could entrust my career. After all, I was betting my work life on it. With that determination, my race to understand my purpose was about to turn into a marathon. Why would the discovery take so long?

---

[2] Dallas Willard, *Renovation of the Heart* (Colorado Springs: NavPress, 2002), p. 248.

First, I had no idea where to begin. I knew of no forum where these questions were discussed in any comprehensive manner. Thus, I adopted a common view of work – "I am an employee". Being an employee is not inherently detrimental to a career. But viewing our work that way is. That framework became a stumbling block to finding the meaning and purpose I bring to my work. I would have been much better off "seeing" myself as a consultant where my present employer is my current client – what value am I bringing to my client rather than what gets me promoted in the company. Of course, rookies often fumble around with the wrong questions and that is typical of a rookie.

Second, the telecommunications industry is so vast that no single person can see and understand it all. It includes equipment manufacturers, network operators, government regulators, investors and billions of customers all distributed around the world. I only got to see a small fraction of it. Working in such a complex industry, I needed a long time to see how my part related to the whole and how my small role mattered.

Third, I didn't get much of a glimpse of the value of my profession early in my career. As researchers in the 1970s, we had no idea how our discoveries would transform society. Not until years later, when I saw how satellite, fiber optics, TCP/IP and other communications technologies made information instantly available everywhere in the world, could I understand the value of my career. Information, I learned, is more powerful than bullets.

Fourth, to be quite honest, I was so involved in inventing my career that my questions got buried in the bottom of my inbox. I was too busy with my own set of issues to truly reflect on the importance of my role. I focused on finding a career that fit my interests, talents and skills. I looked for an invigorating environment that would motivate me. I needed to have an income to support my family. I did not realize at the time that getting paid usually indicates that I am meeting a need in society. I had to make a long series of career course corrections until I found a job with all those attributes. During those decades of navigating my journey and dealing with my personal issues, I never actually looked up to examine the value my work brings to society.

In fact, the course corrections began shortly after I started my first job. The research division of AT&T had a policy of one-person projects. After being in research for five years, I realized that I enjoyed working in teams much more than doing research by myself. In addition, I also enjoyed seeing new technology show up in products. I was not thrilled with simply developing new technology, but preferred seeing it actually incorporated into products used by customers. So I initiated a transfer to a product development organization where I was involved in the newest products. Even though my time in research was productive, it had not been a good fit.

After about six years in the product development organization in AT&T Bell Laboratories, I had a clear sense that the company was going to find it very difficult to operate successfully in the competitive marketplace. I figured it was going to take at least a decade for AT&T to figure out (if ever) how to become a viable competitor. I decided to join a company that already knew how to operate in the competitive marketplace and to avoid all that pain of transforming the culture of AT&T. Even though my experience at AT&T Bell Laboratories had been great, it was no longer a good fit.

In 1981 I joined Racal Data Communications in Florida to head up their advanced technology group for telecommunications products. The company had solid market share and knew how to operate in the competitive market place. Unbeknownst to me, the company was the "cash cow" for starting a mobile telephone company, Vodafone, in the United Kingdom. Vodafone emerged as the world's largest mobile telephone operator, but after about six years, the U.S. affiliate I worked for began to starve to death. After a few rounds of layoffs, I left the company. Even though I learned a great deal about the operations of a commercial company in the competitive market place, my job did not last.

I ended up as head of an engineering organization within the Boeing Company in Seattle. The company decided to start a business unit to design and manufacture products for the telephone industry. After a couple of years, Boeing's executive management abandoned the idea, and senior management placed me in charge of all the communication technology for the aerospace company. It turned out that I am much better suited for the commercial marketplace than the government work I was asked to oversee. My job was no longer a good fit.

In 1990 I was leading a new software design center in Seattle for a telecommunications company in another state. It was the company's first off-site design center. The company eventually consolidated its employees back at its headquarters, and I was laid off. Even though I learned a great deal about managing a client's expectation, my job did not last.

While being laid off, associates within the telecommunications industry began hiring me as a consultant. Due to the highly dynamic nature of the industry and the highly disruptive nature of technology over the intervening 25 years since I started my career, many of my work colleagues were working at a wide range of telecommunications companies all over the world. These people knew me and my expertise and some began to hire me as a consultant. Thus, my consulting business was born. It was not something I had desired to do or ever thought about doing.

But to my amazement, consulting was a great match for me. I loved being highly involved in nothing but critical high-technology projects. I ended up being the chief scientist for multiple clients and becoming part of multiple teams. I no longer dealt with administrative tasks but focused entirely on converting technology into products. I was only invited to meetings that were important for getting my contributions completed. I discovered that the meaning and purpose I bring to work is helping good people succeed. I have been doing it since 1991. I never aspired to be a consultant, but it was a good fit for me.

I was fortunate to have this freedom to invent my career by making this sequence of changes. Many do not. Many, for example, have to pass up a preferred job – or training necessary to pursue their dream career – because it is not compatible with their family circumstances. Individuals can easily be demotivated by having a less than optimal career because they cannot see that the career benefits society. The motivation to make the most of a second-best choice is sometimes hard to generate; but even in these circumstances having a very useful vantage point facilitates finding the meaning and purpose in our work. Even in a second- or third-best situation, the context for work lets us see differently, correspondingly changes how we are creative and eventually leads to work being rewarding.

A couple of decades into my "marathon for meaning" when I was in my late 40s, I crossed the finish line. I finally had enough exposure in the telecommunications industry to see why my industry was important to society. During my career I had a front-row seat for the introduction of the modem, the fax machine, the Internet, voice mail, e-mail, instant messaging, satellites, fiber optics, mobile phones and a growing host of mobile applications. Seeing how these changed the way people operated around the world led me to finally discover the incredible value of telecommunications as seen from a much larger perspective than any single company or organization. This industry brings at least five very important benefits to society:

- **Exposing despots and dictators.** The modem, fax, e-mail, Internet, broadcast satellites and mobile phones make it virtually impossible for despots and dictators to control the flow of information and news within their countries. Without that control, they cannot control the people. Telecommunications makes the world much more aware of what despots and dictators are doing and, thereby, constrains those doing evil. For example, China has tens of thousands of government employees trying to restrict what information its citizens can access on the Internet.

- **Reducing poverty**. Hundreds of millions of people around the world have been lifted out of poverty over the span of my career.[3,4] In almost all cases, the telecommunications infrastructure was an essential component in providing the environment for wealth generation to occur. Although not sufficient on its own, the telecommunications infrastructure is almost always a necessary condition for eliminating poverty.

- **Empowering people**. Prior to the advent of the Internet, most information was locked up in various institutions and only available to the elite people connected to a person within these institutions. Since information is synonymous with power, most people had limited ability for empowerment. Now, the instant availability of vast amounts of information significantly increases the power of ordinary people, whether they live in a giant city or a very small village, are located in a highly developed or an emerging country, or come from a well-connected or disenfranchised family.

---

[3] "Somewhere Over the Rainbow," *The Economist*, Jan. 26, 2008, pp. 27-29.
[4] "Mobile Marvels," Special Report, *The Economist*, Sept. 26, 2009, pp. 1-19.

- **Creating tools for deeper and healthier relationships.** Voice mail, e-mail and mobile phones enhance our ability to develop deep and meaningful friendships. These different modes of communication enrich relationships by adding more dimensions to the way we relate to people. The cost reductions the industry propelled enabled this communications revolution to reach the whole world. Unfortunately, many people use these tools to replace rather than enhance relationships. That is the sad part of being in my profession – to see a tool that could help deepen friendships used to keep relationships superficial or even avoid human contact altogether.

- **Shifting to a world of people, not places.** The advent of e-mail and cell phones fostered in younger people especially a new view of people and geography. Prior to this technology, telephones and mail were connected to the physical place a person lived. Mail was slow and long-distant calls were expensive, so most of our relationships were with people who lived nearby. E-mail has evaporated that notion of place. We can communicate instantaneously and affordably with people around the world. E-mail addresses are names of people, not locations. Our view of community has changed from geography-based to people-based, making us much more people-centric than place-centric. We are expanding our outlook on how relationships grow, with whom and where. Young people are shifting their view of community to an interrelationship of people rather than a neighborhood or even a nation.

What ties these five benefits together? Each improves the lives of people in some tangible way – empowerment, connection, a greater standard of living. Surprisingly, I found that at its foundation the purpose of my work in telecommunications was to care for people. And in helping others, I was actually loving them. Dallas Willard helped me understand this idea of love. Willard says, "Love is the will [my will] to good or 'bene-volence.' We love something or someone when we promote its good for its own sake"[5] This expansive view of what love looks like gave me clarity. I am one of thousands – maybe millions – of technology people generating new products and technology. What we do collectively

---

[5] Dallas Willard, *Renovation of the Heart*, p. 130.

has amazing impact, but my little piece is just as important. I was taken aback by this personal realization that my role matters; it brought incredible meaning to the work I do.

For those of you trying to figure out the importance of your career from the perspective of its benefit to society, I offer the following observations. If I had known earlier in my career what I was experiencing was fairly typical, I might have enjoyed my long journey a lot more than I did.

- **Key answers required patience**. I am sure it is possible to get rock solid answers to my two big questions – Why does my industry matter to society? And why does my involvement in it matter to society? – before age 45, but I don't know anyone who has. Like me, most of us need numerous experiences before we understand the answers well enough that they get internalized.

- **Progress was invisible**. For the first 20-plus years of my career, I felt like all the commitments I made to do excellent work didn't benefit me. I was building industry-specific skills, developing solid business values, developing leadership style, making significant contributions and earning the respect of my peers. Some of my accomplishments received significant recognition. I valued the judgments of my peers and bosses and used their feedback to move forward with encouragement or to make course corrections. However, I knew that my engine was not yet firing on all cylinders. I felt unsettled. Of all the areas of my life, this long period of development demanded a blind commitment from me. I had no way to know that simply focusing on excellence in my work would get me to the future I was anticipating. During this period, since I had no assurance or evidence that I was on a good path, I lived with much anxiety about the future. It drained a good portion of my creative energy.

- **I had few companions in this adventure**. When I chose to enter the technical world, I found very few people with the experience, skills and wisdom to know how to encourage me in my search for meaning at work. I was not prepared for how lonely the adventure would be. I kept my eye out for others on a similar journey. I ultimately met a handful of business leaders who operate with high values and solid ethics. By carefully observing them, I learned and was encouraged by their example.

- **I was very surprised when all my dues were paid and my career took off.** When the answers to my two key questions came, I was pleasantly surprised at the passion unleashed within me and the opportunities that came my way. The previous 20-plus years that appeared as insignificant had actually created in me technical competency, a solid character and an understanding of what to care about. I needed these capabilities when my career suddenly took off and raced forward with increasing speed. Opportunities for making significant contributions to society seemingly appeared out of nowhere. One major avenue for this is my consulting business, which I began in 1991. Once I grabbed hold of what already existed, my consulting business flourished.

These qualities of competency, character and caring kept my focus in the right place and prevented me from being seduced by my career. We all have seen some mighty oak trees felled at the pinnacle of a career because poor character created shallow roots. We have seen people fumble the ball because of insufficient competency. And we have watched others fail to lead a team because they cared only about their own interests, not that of the entire team. In the coming chapters we'll look at the importance of these three traits in being a player when it comes to contributing to society – caring about people through the products and services we produce.

I was so caught up in just navigating the course of my career, that I did not take the time to seek and adopt a viable and robust "vantage point" from which to view my career. Viewing myself as an employee, I futilely tried to create a place for myself in the company where I worked. If I had viewed my career as "being in business for myself" where my present employer is my current client, I would have had a much easier time finding answers in that context than in the one I had. Much later I found a very rich context within which to find the unique answers that suited me. The remainder of the book describes a vantage point from which we have an easier time uncovering the hidden treasure in our work. That vantage point has enough comprehensive content and nuance to match with reality – it can hold our weight. We can entrust our career to it.

Tradesman Keeps Equipment Humming

Darvin was struggling with how he could provide financially for his family. He had no thought that one day he would have so much enjoyment seeing the smile on a customer's face when he fixed a machine that got the business running again.

By Mr. Darvin Avis

I'm a tradesman, the owner of a one-stop machinery repair company, whose career path started in high school when I showed a greater curiosity for mechanics than academics. As my friends headed to college, I enrolled in an automotive mechanic course. Before they graduated, I had already worked for Chrysler, General Motors and Caterpillar dealerships. So who could have guessed that I would spend much of the next 40 years taking classes and passing arduous certification tests to gain the expertise I needed to do my job and, ultimately, lead me to a career I love?

I started my career in Seattle in 1970 just as the region's main employer, Boeing, began a horrendous downsizing and work by Caterpillar on the Alaska pipeline was delayed. The economic times were awful for many people, especially an apprentice mechanic. A now-famous billboard expressed a common discouragement: "Will the last person leaving Seattle please turn out the lights?" If I had any hope of finding a job, I would need to take the initiative.

I met a person who knew of an opening at a knitting company, and I pursued the lead. After getting the job, the first thing one of the owners asked me was, "Know anything about machinery?" Even though I didn't, I spent the next five years programming and repairing the knitting production machinery made in Switzerland, Germany and Spain.

The company soon had an opening for a licensed boiler operator, so I pursued that job as well. I reached a deal with the managers. The company would pay for 40 hours of classroom teaching, and I would perform the mandatory 80 hours of hands-on boiler room training on my own time. I was now a car mechanic, machine repairman and a boiler operator.

My resume may have been growing, but I was not making enough money to support my family. I had to figure out a road to better-paying jobs. I went after more licenses. On my own time and at my own expense, I studied and passed the test for the next higher boiler grade – the Steam Engineer license. On my own time and at my own expense, I earned a Refrigeration Operating Engineer license. I was willing to master any craft that I thought could provide me with consistent income.

With all my licenses in hand, I got a job as an engineer at a large bakery. During my five years there, the bakery doubled in size from one city block to two. It was full of equipment, some 15 feet high with a quarter mile of conveyers. With the expansion came a new 400-horsepower boiler. Still looking for ways to become more valuable to my employer – and possibly earn more money in the process – I volunteered to work toward adding a Boiler Supervisor Endorsement onto my Steam Engineer license. I was giving them more than a full day's work for a full day's pay by earning the licenses the government required on my own time.

I was part of a great crew and was learning how to repair many different kinds of machinery. I loved the ingenuity it took to solve the complex electromechanical problems that kept the production line moving, even if we were waiting for the replacement parts to arrive. I knew that we played a key role in making the business succeed.

During my time at the bakery, I came to realize that I wanted more ownership over my career. I wanted my own clients and more control of my future, so I left the bakery to work with a friend who owned a heating company. He agreed to let me start my own company while I worked with him. I began to pursue my own boiler and bakery machinery repair accounts. And once again, I realized I would need a higher grade boiler license – the Grade One Steam Engineer – to master more crafts and bring more value to my customers. Even with the license, I was struggling financially. My wife often made more money in a week babysitting for three children than I did with my clients. We were still in survival mode.

My next hurdle came in 1983 when I decided to pursue an Electrical Administrator license. After a two-year struggle in which I took the exam five times and eventually filed a grievance letter with the state of Washington highlighting what I thought were improprieties in the testing process, I passed the exam. Darvin Electric, Inc. could actually do some wiring.

My accounts continued to grow, and I launched my own company, completely independent of other employers. With my automotive engine knowledge, mechanical repair knowledge, boiler and steam licenses, and electrician licenses, I became a one-stop machinery repair company offering electrical, mechanical, internal combustion engine, and heating and air conditioning services. I could get equipment back on line quickly because I didn't need to bring in other tradesmen to do small pieces of the work.

These were still survival years. I was committed to doing excellent work, so I could gain good references and repeat business and build a financial cushion that could get me through any unexpected downturns. By the late 1990s my company was finally strong financially, and I noticed a big change in my attitude. I stopped looking for what I could get from my customers and began to really enjoy what I could give them: reliable repairs in the shortest time possible at the lowest cost. My service motto had become, "I would rather be a hero than a zero."

Every day when the phone rings and the caller explains his equipment troubles, I rise to the challenge. I anticipate the relief on the face and shoulders of the hotel facilities manager when I get his boiler back on line and all his guests will have the hot showers they expect. I know the baker will smile after I fix her 100-foot oven. I want to see the head chef's frustration disappear when I get his fryer operating and he can finish his chicken orders. Meeting my customers' needs has become an invigorating motivation for me. I never tire of diagnosing the problem, discovering an elegant solution. It's a great reward for the decades I spent simply trying to pay the bills.

I also enjoy finally having stable enough work that allows me to turn off my phone each night from midnight to 8:00 a.m. Forty years ago, the Boeing "bust" propelled me to focus on mastering new and necessary crafts. I spent many years studying and taking exams and consumed with trying to pay my bills, but now I have landed in a place where I can truly enjoy keeping my clients' machinery humming along and making their businesses successful. Nothing beats the smile on the baker's face as he gets back to making "dough" after I get the commercial oven back on line.

Products and Services: People First – Section II

An Avenue for Caring About People

Through our very different journeys, Darvin Avis and I both arrived at the same understanding of the purposes of our career: Our role in business was to care about people by providing them with products and services they value. Our journeys had another thing in common: a sense that we often had very few people to reveal the bigger framework and encourage us through our many career disappointments and decisions.

Research suggests that this lack of purpose is common. In their examination of prestigious U.S. business schools, authors Rakesh Khurana and Herbert Gintis failed to find one that could explain the purpose of business in society with enough inspiration to fuel a person's 30- to 40-year career. They wrote:

> There is no universally understood role, no explicit focus on, or discussion about what an MBA means to the profession or to society as a whole.... If someone asks our students to pinpoint business's true mission, we want them to have a compelling answer.[6]

Interestingly, the authors do not give a very compelling answer themselves. But at least they know the question needs an answer and are dealing with the problem.

We might get a glimpse of inspiration into the importance of our careers from the practice of commissioning church members for special service projects. I knew about a man who was going to a village in Africa for two weeks to help dig a well. His work would provide disease-free water in a part of the world where, according to the World Health Organization, unsafe water can be traced to 80 percent of the illnesses afflicting residents and where 400 people an hour die of cholera and

---

[6] Rakesh Khurana and Herbert Gintis, "What Is the Purpose of Business?" *BizEd*, January/February 2008, pp. 54-55.

other water-borne diseases. Church members understood that the project would save lives, and they sent the man off with their support.

Is there a way to similarly encourage people who work for the water company right in our own community? These workers do the same thing as the church member – provide clean water to people – and are likely to stay at it up to 40 years, not just two weeks. They go to work each day to maintain a complex system that makes sure our water flows every time someone turns on the faucet, 24 hours a day 7 days a week. They plan for the future, making sure we have enough water not only today but also as our population grows. They test the water every day to ensure it meets all health standards. Has anyone helped them understand the importance of their career?

More often, I suspect, we spend far more time questioning the work ethic of our city employees than appreciating the health we enjoy because of them. They are an integral part of the delivery system for meeting people's most basic needs. Far from simply earning a living, what these workers do result in caring for their neighbors – us. After all they are saving us from dying of cholera, doing the job so well we do not even notice any more!

Sometimes the needs met by various businesses aren't as basic or don't seem as obvious, but all honest industry cares for people in some way. At its core, business creates wealth for a community and elevates the standard of living for its residents. We obviously cannot help lift people out of poverty unless we create wealth faster than we create people. It is very simple mathematics. If the world's population is growing faster than the world's wealth, then people are getting poorer. Only business can create wealth – governments, educational institutions and non-profit organizations can facilitate healthy businesses but cannot create wealth on that scale. Their funding depends on the wealth generated by business.

Admittedly, wealth creation is only the first step in developing a comprehensive solution to poverty. Distributing that wealth appropriately is another key issue. While that issue is beyond the scope of this book, some progress is being made. *The Economist* reports that more than 1.2 billion people were added to the middle class from 1990 to 2005, almost doubling the size of the world's middle class.[7]

Closely linked to global poverty is world hunger. To solve world hunger, we must first produce enough food at a cheap enough price (efficiently) for everyone to afford it. It takes a vast army of people to do that – the hybrid seed scientist, agronomist, botanist, fertilizer producer, farm equipment manufacturer, transportation industry, steel industry, petrochemical industry, financier, refrigeration industry, market trader, truck driver, road worker, ship crew, train crew, retail sales staff, lawmaker, lawyer, etc., etc., etc. Only business can make all the pieces come together efficiently enough on the worldwide scale necessary to meet the overwhelming need.

The end result of food getting to hungry people is facilitated or inhibited by the people and the systems that distribute it. When all professions are doing their job well, people benefit. But when greed and corruption (character failings) distort industries or government agencies, the system fails or is greatly crippled. A healthy society demands government and business leaders of strong competency and character who care about the right purposes and priorities.

The production and delivery system

We don't have to feed starving people or deliver safe water to have a sense of dignity that our work meets people's needs and really matters. Consider the fastener industry, for example. We don't want the operating room lamps to fall apart when we are in surgery. We don't want the airplane to come apart when we are flying. When fasteners do their job, we don't even think about the factory worker who makes the nails and screws, bolts and rivets, solders and welds, and tapes and adhesives in the products we use every day.

The products and services of the vast majority of businesses have a noble purpose similar to the lowly fastener and play a key role in caring for – in loving – others. Deeply caring about people's needs, it turns out, provides the answer to vexing question posed by authors Khurana and Gintis: What is the purpose of business? Looking at business from a larger perspective, the providers of products and services meet the needs of customers and, thus, care deeply about people. In the process of

---

[7] "Burgeoning Bourgeoise: A Special Report on the New Middle Classes in Emerging Markets", *The Economist*, Feb. 14, 2009, p. 4.

delivering products and services we also benefit employees, suppliers and investors – more people.

Business benefits people

It is very easy to miss that the purpose of business is to care deeply about people's needs because business speaks a different language. Business goes straight to the means: sales quotas, production efficiency, rapid product development, return on investment, cost controls, etc. Often, this focus on the means results in using and manipulating colleagues rather than taking them on a higher-purpose adventure. The means is important but misses its deeper and rarely stated purpose: caring about people, all people – customers, employees, management, suppliers and investors. Ethical people might operate with this purpose because of their personal values, but I am advocating a broader view. Without major proactive measures to remind us that business is all about meeting people's needs, we slowly lose our bearings.

We also lose our bearings if we place more importance on our work than it deserves. Work is important, but it is not the most important aspect of life. A value system that puts people first at work also helps us order our priorities outside the office. We choose to give the right attention to all the people and responsibilities in our lives, starting with the most important – our spouse and families – then friends and, lastly, career. This ranked set of priorities provides a basis for making decisions when conflicting demands arise. On several occasions, I have had to choose between getting a project done on time or attending one of my children's sporting events. I was willing to miss a weekly game here and there, but missing my son's high school state championship football game was not an option.

We often spend more time with people at work than with those who are more important to us, but time is not the means of evaluating how well we are living our priorities. The ranked priorities of spouse, family, friends and then work provide a mechanism to make the decisions at work based on all the relationships in our life. Thus, decisions on how to invest our time reside solely within the realm of relationships. We still have to make tough choices. But at least the choices exist in the domain of relationships and do not consist of a mixture of relationships and other factors. Such a mixture would make decisions all the more complex. Moreover, all the choices we make reflect the relationships that are most important to us. Thus, we end up with more freedom to act.

Typically, we are encouraged to "balance" family and career, an idea that suggests the two compete for our attention and one drains energy from the other. Instead I recommend we "integrate" marriage, family, friends and career, creating a synergism that provides greater fuel for all relationships. Integration is not a simple task. It takes extensive creative thinking and initiative that is beyond the scope of our topic. As Stephen R. Covey, in his book *First Things First,* says about family and work, "It's not 'either/or,' it's 'and.'"[8] This integration of our life is well worth doing. It benefits all our relationships and every aspect of our careers.

The work most of us do ultimately benefits people. When we see our careers in this context, the purpose and meaning of our work becomes apparent. It is much easier to value and enjoy our everyday work. Even the drudgery in any job does not seem to weigh us down so heavily.

---

[8] Stephen R. Covey, *First Things First,* (New York City, Simon and Schuster, 1994), Chapter 6.

Accounting Liberates People in Developing Countries

Serena Morones, a certified public accountant, worked in several humanitarian projects in Africa before she realized that a critically essential key to unlocking the economic development of the entire country is accounting.

By Ms. Serena Morones

People don't often consider the role of accountants in changing the world. But since I have been in Rwanda and witnessed a huge number of Westerners get involved in starting or supporting businesses there, I have also seen impediments to that investing/giving. Two of the biggest investment impediments are 1) lack of reliable information flowing back to the investor and 2) lack of trust with money (fear of fraud/corruption). Both of these problems are caused in part by poor accounting.

Let me back up and share a little about my views on economic development. I don't think that most people will have success with micro loans, the small loans designed to help people start their own businesses and lift themselves out of poverty. Most people in the world do not have the aptitude to run their own business. They are destined to be employees, not entrepreneurs. Developing countries need industry, such as manufacturing, in order to create jobs for the average citizen. That industry will require substantial foreign investment initially, yet there remain huge impediments to that investment.

Western investors rightly require information about the prospects of their investment followed by reliable ongoing information about how the investment is performing. They will not pour funds into a black hole of mystery. Yet investors oftentimes cannot get the information they need to keep their projects going or help them stay healthy.

Another impediment to foreign investment is a concern over corruption. Corruption is fostered, in part, by an absence of accountability and correct information. When a project installs basic accounting practices along with fundamental internal controls, the likelihood of corruption decreases dramatically.

One of the biggest American investors in Rwanda said to me that if there were one thing he could do to change the investment climate in Rwanda, it would be to release an army of trained accountants.

African students probably do not know the value of becoming an accountant or the tremendous job security they could have. I see students choosing careers that they can identify around them, and African youth don't see many prosperous accountants. To serve as an accountant in Rwanda and to train young men and women in accounting might be work at its best.

Long Road to Finding Meaning

How did Charlie, who did all he could to avoid working, end up caring about workers who pay too little attention to their fair treatment in the work place?

By Mr. Charlie Glendinning

I was dragged kicking and screaming into the workforce. I lived in a wild neighborhood full of joyous children for whom work was a four-letter word. It was soulless, sweating drudgery that ended with the grim awareness of a lost day and further compounded by the fact that it would all have to be done again the next week. I felt a kinship with Sisyphus, who was eternally doomed to a life of futility, the stone he rolled up the hill always rolling down just before it reached the top.

My mother saw things differently. She was on a quest to instill in me the higher virtues of duty, honor, justice, courage, commitment and reverence that came every Saturday through shovels, rakes, mowers and hoes. I was a prisoner of the Puritan work ethic looking for every possible means of escape.

Fast-forward 50 years and I still mourn Saturdays but for a different reason. As much as I love all the joys and spontaneity that the weekends have to offer, I wish the workweek hadn't ended so quickly. Far from being blue, my Mondays fill me with excitement, optimism and anticipation. Why the change? I kept rolling stones to the top of the hill, where they eventually stayed and I was able to build a foundation for a career that I love, one in which my talents and personality can play at least a small part in improving the lives of our country's workforce. The journey was rocky, beginning with the day near the end of high school when I told my father I wanted to be an artist.

To his credit, he remained quite calm. His face didn't twitch, his eyes didn't flutter, yet the effect of my pronouncement on his analytical, mathematical, scientific brain (genetically endowed from his father and further shaped and hardened by four years at the Naval Academy and four years in the Marine Corps, two of them in the Korean War) was palpable. I waited for his armor to crack.

29

To my father's credit, he swallowed the words that had risen in his throat and said instead, "You *do* have quite an eye for art." Just as I began to relax, he added, "But you know there are and have been many starving artists in the world. Van Gogh never sold a painting in his lifetime. What do you think of trying commercial art? Your grandfather was a photographer but he also started an advertising company and made a pretty good living at it." Still guiding. Still molding. Still shaping.

I could see his point. Money talks. At least it began speaking to me. So I enrolled in the graphic arts program at Virginia Commonwealth University where I soon discovered how much I hated my chosen profession, the one that seemed so logical and reasonable the day I talked with my father. The precision, the attention to detail, the need to color within the lines. All were, in the words of Hamlet, the slings and arrows of my outrageous fortune in Graphic Arts 101. This was no place to attack a canvas with wild colors, to experiment with flamboyant technique, to paint when you felt like it and stop when you didn't. There were deadlines, grades, processes and procedures, all stifling my creativity. After two years I took arms against my sea of troubles and ended my college studies.

I went to work for a printing company, which forced me to see my graphics training from the other side. At college I was struggling with the input side. Here I began to see that precision and attention to detail were so important for a beautiful output. I fell in love with typography and creative ways it could be used. Seeing the world of graphic arts from the opposite direction gave me the perspective I was meant to have all along.

After gaining valuable printing and design skills, I took a job with the American Federation of Teachers, a teachers' union affiliated with the AFL-CIO. Are you keeping track of my mistakes to this point? First, I wanted to be an artist. Second, I dropped out of school. Third, the son of a conservative Republican veteran went to work for an organization created in 1916, around the time of the Russian revolution. Coincidence? Not to my family. But I wanted to further my art, and the AFT seemed to have a heart for the well-being of its people.

That was 35 years ago, and I'm still there. It's taken me that long to understand my various relationships to work as well as its relationship to me. My first realization was that I have a basic *need* to work. Apart from any good I do or money I earn, I get depressed when I am perfectly, utterly lazy, when I waste something of value: my time. Even though I've been out from under the watchful and sometimes harassing eye of my parents for years, I find myself making lists for Saturday and Sunday and sensing great joy and peace as I cross each item off. Could it be that my mother had been right all along, that *some* of the soulless drudgery I endured might be virtues in disguise?

This first relationship to work seems to be both a visceral and innate desire to work. Rather than toil, work fulfills a deep desire to be alive and active.

My second realization was that when I work, I get money. I can buy things I need, like food and shelter, as well as things I don't, like computers and ice cream and Redskins tickets. This second discovery came at about the time I got married and began a family. I was starting to become more outwardly focused and to realize how my *desire* to work had developed into a *responsibility*. My paycheck became the focus for discussion and debate. How could we divide it up in such a way to provide for everyone in the family – all our needs and as many wants as we could afford? We began to develop a more mature way of thinking about work and how we could use it to spread love in our little but brave new world. Yet it was still a bit self-centered and lacked a grander purpose.

The third realization of my work outlook took the longest to take root in my heart. After working at the AFT for about 20 years, I began to truly connect with the work we did. I'd come to love and admire the people we serve. Besides organizing teachers and para-teachers, the AFT organizes nurses, public employees and college professors. These people wrestle on the frontlines of an ongoing battle between their sense of calling to their profession and those in authority over them. As hard as it is to imagine teachers, nurses and public employees united under a common cause, this sense of calling unites all of them.

I have seen countless examples of a manager or administrator who knows of a person's passion for her job and purposely exploits that passion. They know that the person who enters one of these fields has a heart of service, and that a desire to help often leaves them vulnerable to extra demands or manipulation. People with hearts burning for those they serve can become blind to issues of proper work and personal boundaries. They need advocates, and I am proud to work for an organization whose job it is to open the eyes of the people on both sides of the table.

So it is, finally, that I've come to realize that when *who* it is we work for supplants personal gain or personal desire, any suffering under the curse of toil is minimized – sometimes even eclipsed – by wanting the best for those we serve. This mindset makes work not just bearable but deeply meaningful and satisfying. In answer to Hamlet's famous question, I very much have found my reason to be.

Discovering an Integrated Life

What did it take for Michelle to navigate the journey of integrating a fragmented life into a coherent life where she now enjoys seeing her efforts at work make a difference to those for whom she labors?

By Ms. Michelle DeYoung

Following a dramatic faith experience I had as a teenager, my world split into two very clear compartments: the sacred and the secular. Clearly, the sacred world of faith, relationships and charity was far superior to the secular world of business and commerce. My life, therefore, became a pursuit of the sacred and a disdain for the secular. I began to see everything in life as good or bad, a dichotomy that set me up for a crash and forced me to put my life and career in a completely new context.

I moved to Washington, DC, after college and had no trouble finding like-minded friends. We talked about faith and community and wondered how to integrate them into all aspects of our lives. In this circle of friends I met the man who would become my husband. How ironic that his interests lay in the marts of commerce and that we chose to move to London. He started a business and I enrolled in graduate school.

At the London School of Economics, I began to be equipped with the knowledge and skills to fulfill my purpose in the marketplace. I was surrounded by stimulating people from many nations who were pursuing excellence in their disciplines as well as their relationships and in some cases their faith. We had endless discussions over copious amounts of coffee and cigarettes into the wee small hours of the morning. As all of our ideas came under scrutiny, the wall between my sacred and secular compartments began to crack.

What shattered instead was my marriage. After my first semester my husband left me, leaving my carefully crafted view of the sacred in a million pieces. Cut by the shards, I began to examine every relationship I saw. I longed for the restoration of my sacred marriage and my simpler-to-understand compartmentalized life.

We did not reconcile but I took my first trepid steps forward, still clinging to my disparate worldview. I moved to Spain to be near my brother (sacred) and learn a second language to help me succeed in the global community (secular). I taught commercial English to leaders of vast enterprises (secular). I learned about different industries and how they functioned (secular). A friend from my DC days (sacred) hired me to analyze potential ventures in Europe for the Australian government (secular). I carefully judged each career step while clinging to the unspoken hope that one day I would be able to return to my former life and fulfill my greater purpose.

My greater purpose, it turns out, was not in the past. It continued to unfold in the world of business. While visiting the United States, I met a man who understood my struggle between the sacred and secular and shared with me how he had bridged that gap and now lives out his passions and purpose in his consulting business. Within six months, I joined his firm, where I have remained to this day. To live fully in the world of business and to hold on to the passion I have always had for the sacred has not been easy. However, the opportunity to be mentored and equipped for the marketplace (secular) to fulfill my passion and purpose (sacred) has been crucial to my journey.

I spent time with a South African couple who showed me how the Bible contains the foundation for the best practices, tools and techniques at the heart of many of today's businesses. I have joined teams and worked in developing countries to help small and medium-sized businesses adopt these principles and practices to create sustainable businesses. On the ground, we partner with local consultants and spend several weeks walking through an operating model with our clients. The results are transformational, both for the clients and for our team.

On one particular trip, as my late night flight departed from a city 9,000 miles away from home, I knew that my paradigm had finally shifted. The sacred and secular were no longer separate. I realized that the way I operate makes no distinction between the two. What does this integration look like?

Ultimately, I discovered that relationships are important wherever you are. I can trace every major business achievement to an agreement by those involved to work together. While working with a major healthcare provider in the United States, two traditional adversaries (union and management) chose to focus on their common interests, rather than their disagreements. A transformation took place. One work group identified cost savings of $89.5 million over three years. One hospital improved operating room efficiency by 50 percent. Another reduced wait time from 60 to 20 minutes and increased patient satisfaction to 90 percent.

The value I place on relationships also determines how I spend my time and money. If I value people above all else, I will invest my time in them. If I value material gain above all else, my time will be dedicated to achieving that. It's a simple equation in which my behavior, not my words, reveals my true values.

This respect for people is the foundation for an integrated worldview as well as the bedrock of my consulting work. One of our firm's core beliefs is that if we equip people with the right skills, knowledge, education and tools to do their job and we give them an understanding of their role in the business and the context for the business, then they will almost always make the right decision. I have seen this borne out time and again. It's not to say that employees don't make mistakes or that they don't make wrong decisions. We are, after all, human. But their intentions are usually good, and they are willing to learn from their mistakes.

As I spend the majority of my days in what I once considered the secular world of business, I feel that I am in the most sacred place I can be. I no longer long for things of the past. There is not a better life to go back to, a more sacred, significant and meaningful existence. This is my life. As I seek to be as authentic as possible with every person I encounter, I am doing what I am called to do. Whether my work takes me abroad or keeps me at home, whether it is volunteer or highly compensated, I do not use these as yardsticks with which to measure its value. My yardstick is whether I spent my time and resources to help and love people at work and in my personal life. That's what will endure. It's the sacred and secular integrated in all that I do and all that I am that truly matters.

Pastor Soars in Two Careers

As both a pilot and a pastor, John ultimately discovered that he had the same purpose for doing both.

By Mr. John Gilman

In the fifth grade, I had to write down my father's occupation on a family history form. I asked my mom what I should put down, and after a thoughtful pause, she said, "Laborer." I greatly loved and respected my dad, but I could tell from her response that a laborer wasn't highly regarded.

The problem wasn't just its lower-middle-class status. It was also the secular nature of his work. In my world, shaped by the leaders and friends at our Christian church, the greatest work was to spread our faith. This view implied there were two levels of occupations: first, eternally important jobs relating to God and, below that, the okay but relatively unimportant, normal jobs in the world. There were even rankings within this ranking. At the top of the faith-related jobs were missionaries and evangelists. In the rest of the world, health care professionals and scientists led the list. I had a pretty good idea that laborers were near the bottom.

As a young person, I was encouraged to see if God was calling me to "full-time Christian service." And I was willing to see if he was. I enrolled at Willamette University in Salem, Oregon, and moved into a Christian discipleship house with a group of guys committed to "reaching Oregon." We would tell people about Jesus and ask them to commit their lives to him, with the ultimate goal of making sure everyone in Oregon heard and responded to our Christian message.

My enthusiasm was soon tested. I was enrolled in Air Force ROTC, and I got so excited about flying that I put reaching Oregon on hold and left to reach the skies in the Oregon Air National Guard. My guard unit sent me to the Air Force's Aviation Cadet Program to be trained as an officer and pilot. I loved the entire experience – the challenges, discipline, standards of excellence and first-class flight training.

After returning to the Reach Oregon team 18 months later, I continued to fly. My team on the ground worked across the state to tell the people of Oregon about Jesus, and gathered one weekend a month to play, pray and share our lives. My team in the air flew fighter-interceptors for the Air National Guard. I loved both worlds: my band of brothers trying to save Oregon spiritually and my other band of men defending America from Soviet bombers.

I married and then we started our own discipleship house and I went "full-time" in the ministry, although I kept flying in the Guard. Unfortunately, neither of these worlds brought in much money. My wife, Jeanah, and I lived on so little that one man remarked that his insurance premiums were more than our income. One winter, following the birth of our first child, we had to go without heat. We would buy a little firewood when we could and kept our baby near the fire. We decided I needed to get a job. I tried – mostly unsuccessfully – selling cars, selling bookkeeping services, eventually becoming a firefighter. In my free time, I continued my ministry work. Then the Air National Guard lured me back for another mission.

My guard unit needed men for a six-month secret mission on the B-57, a small two-engine bomber. We didn't know where we were going or what we would do but I thought it would be great to fly to other places in the world. It was 1962, and I was assigned to a spook-and-reconnaissance unit that participated in President Kennedy's atomic test program on Christmas Island on the equator south of Hawaii. Our job was to fly through the mushroom clouds of the blasts and gather air samples of the material in the cloud for scientists to analyze. I was checked for radiation after each flight and I never considered our mission dangerous (I was 25 years old).

When I returned home, I was ready to live a more normal life as a husband and father with a steady job and income. My ideas of work had shifted. I was on my journey of discovering that what a person does at home and work contributes as much to the world good in its way as the ministry does in its way. So I quit my leadership role with the discipleship house and eventually became a pilot for TWA.

As I worked for TWA my thinking evolved about the nature and importance of work. The lessons came in unexpected ways. I recalled one from years earlier in pilot training: One day a young airman who maintained the grass on the air base made the most amazing statement about his job. He said his work was important because the pilots needed the runways to be free of blowing dust. I was touched. His dignity came from helping me do my job. I came to see that my dignity came from helping the U.S. air defense – and later from safely and reliably flying people to their destinations as a pilot for TWA as well as from training other TWA pilots to do the same.

That's not why I became a pilot in the first place, to provide a good service to the world. I did it because it was fun. And I was good at it. Over time I was able to understand the benefits it brought to others and to shift my thinking to believe that most careers fit in with God. I see the great good of the work done by health care professionals, scientists, college professors, managers, craftsmen, tradesmen, laborers, attorneys and IRS agents. Are some of these occupations more important than others? Is the hard-working owner of the paper mill more important than the laborer because he employs many laborers? Is the food grower more important than the paper producer? Is the agricultural scientist more important than the food grower? In the same way my church ranked the importance of ministry jobs, our society is quick to rank secular professions. The doctor outranks the nurse, the nurse outranks the aide, the aide outranks the janitor. Yet all these jobs are necessary for good patient care. Some require more knowledge, some more strength. But all contribute to a patient's wellbeing.

Many people don't have the luxury of choice – they'd like to be the surgeon but circumstances land them in the hospital kitchen. They still can choose to work with joy, to understand the good that their dishwashing skills are doing.

A leader in the faith once urged me to leave flying and return to full-time ministry. He said many people could fly but not many could minister. I didn't believe that I should quit flying. I was doing good work as a pilot, and I believed that the way Jesus lived most of his adult life – as a laborer – is how most of us are called to live ours. My avocation was – and still is – firmly planted in the church. I consider the church to be the most effective and easiest way to care for people's spiritual and relational needs, and I have served as a lay pastor most of my adult life. But I also consider the work that most of us do 40-50 hours a week a God-given calling. When we understand how our work produces good for others, we understand the great purpose of our work. It's a blessing I wish my parents had enjoyed.

Multiple Playing Fields – Section III
Vast Majority of Occupations Contribute

Although I focus most of the attention on the business world where I spent my entire career, other segments of society have many of the same attributes. They too are part of the delivery system for meeting people's basic needs and contributing to their well being. The people who work in government, education and non-profit sectors of society have critical roles to fill. The vantage point for viewing our work applies equally well to these careers and avocations.

Effective government provides a level playing field for business opportunities and enforces the rule of law. It allows business to flourish. It keeps bad people at bay – whether they are powerful companies trying to monopolize markets or thugs who rob and murder people – while allowing as much freedom as possible. Needed regulation goes hand in hand with healthy capitalism. Effective regulation fosters transparency of business governance and limits greed.

Corrupt government breeds corrupt and dysfunctional businesses by rewarding dishonest businesspeople and giving them significant competitive advantages. When government officials take bribes to ignore building codes, buildings collapse in hurricanes or earthquakes and people die. When regulators are on the take, timber companies rape the land or investment management companies steal people's money. When officials can be bought off, companies exploit and enslave employees and ignore child labor laws. Corrupt government rewards corrupt businesses at the cost of honest businesses. Businesses that benefit people cannot flourish when government workers are corrupt. The same is true for governments that are incompetent or uncaring.

Government includes a host of services – libraries, parks, fire protection, zoning, transportation, schools, military, roads, waterways, flood control, airports, ports, building codes, public health and food preparation inspection. The judicial system helps to enforce the laws of business. The courts' role is varied, from punishing dishonest practices to preventing the government from being too heavy-handed.

41

Equally important is education, which plays a key role in developing competency in people for all roles within businesses, families and society. Education amplifies our ability to love others by honing our raw talent and interest into deployable skills. Democracy counts on an educated citizenry to be aware of the issues, elect honest civic leaders and ensure that laws do not exploit others.

Education also provides a path out of poverty. The availability of high-quality education for all children is a huge prerequisite for a vigorous life. Education comes in many forms, including public, private, youth, adult, non-profit, for-profit, classroom, video documentaries and on-line classes.

Training, unlike a general education program, prepares a person for a particular task or job. The apprenticeship of a plumber or electrician trains the person, as does student teaching for teachers and residency for physicians. Most employees receive training at work to do their jobs.

Non-profit organizations fill roles not serviced effectively by business or government, particularly true in the areas of social services, the arts and public policy. Think tanks provide critical thinking, position papers and advocacy for numerous public policy issues. International relief organizations get goods and services directly to needy people in ways that government agencies cannot. Civic organizations provide avenues for people to invest in their communities. Non-profits that fill a wide array of needs include hospitals, clinics, family foundations, churches, social agencies, professional societies, museums, theaters, symphonies, zoos, youth organizations and sport clubs.

Paid careers in business, government, education and the non-profits are not the only contributors to society. Avocations and non-paid vocations are equally important when seen from the perspective of their impact on society. When money for living comes from another source, people have the luxury of a wider set of choices for how to invest their time "working." For example, stay-at-home parents can invest full-time in their children's lives and world. They – like the paid members of society – might also choose to spend free hours volunteering in all kinds of organizations: from schools to athletics, local government to church, or environmental groups to civic organizations. Like business careers, these avocations are another part of society's delivery system for meeting people's needs.

Clearly my experience resides entirely within the industrial world of high technology. But just as clearly the framework that work is all about people is just as equally at home in other segments of society. The remainder of the book demonstrates that we can trust the framework to find our purpose for our work no matter in what segment of society your job happens to be.

Choosing our career

We are born with a unique set of talents, skills and interests. Why not choose a career because some aspect of it interests us and draws us in? Why not choose work we enjoy? Some might try to stifle that passion with advice to devote our life to some good cause that we don't care as much about. The most effective pastors, pilots and grocers enjoy their jobs. There is plenty of tedious work in any profession without deliberately choosing one you don't like. It probably does not matter which career or vocation we choose. We need to choose and get about pursuing it.

In today's industrialized countries, we have the opportunity to work where we can find the best fit for our innate skills and interests. This opportunity to choose is a very recent phenomenon in our history and still is not available to most people in the developing world. And even in the developed world many face circumstances that do not allow them to maximize their potential. However, even if we have been forced into a second or third choice for a career because of life's circumstances, our work has dignity and noble purpose if we observe it from the larger context or perspective.

Home as a Launching Pad

Gwen changed the context from which she saw her marriage and family. It dramatically transformed both.

By Ms. Gwen Barrett

Iral was my high school sweetheart, and we were married very young. We gave little thought to life goals. All we wanted to do was enjoy each other and get Iral through college. He worked and went to school, and I cared for our home and family. Because we had so little money, I took pleasure in learning how to make something out of nothing. Orange crates became bedside tables. I sewed our clothes or bought them at the thrift store. Food was gleaned and canned and often meager. We lived in small rented spaces that required all my creativity to turn into a warm, welcoming home.

Iral and I both desired to be people of generous hearts. Even though we had very little money, from the very first day of our marriage we agreed to give at least 10 percent of our income to those in need. This giving became foundational to our view of money and developed an attitude of thankfulness, even during those years when we had little. When Iral graduated with a master's degree, we had a good marriage, two children and no debt.

With Iral employed full time, our finances improved, but our budget was still tight. I had several opportunities to work outside the home but, after figuring the cost of a work wardrobe, childcare, transportation and other expenses, my net income always turned out to be about $10 a month. That was no reason for me to leave home. Even though I stayed at home because of financial considerations and loved caring for my family, I desired to make a difference in the world. As a homemaker, I was purposing to each day do my tasks with diligence, but daily preparing dinner for my family wasn't enough to feed my soul. I had to find deeper meaning in my chosen occupation.

So I chose to open my front door. If I couldn't be out in the world, I would invite the world inside. I couldn't have predicted who would show up and what they would teach me. I found myself caring for others in the

45

ordinary ways I cared for my family, even inviting some to move in with us. I developed friendships that challenged many of my ideas and encouraged me to embrace the significance of my role. This growing desire and ability to care for others spilled over into my family. I became committed to helping my children discover a purpose and direction for their lives. Our home became a launching place.

Iral and I had gotten involved with Young Life, an organization focused on high school students, when we moved to Salem, Oregon, after graduate school. We opened our home for weekly meetings, we gave financial support, and we encouraged the various Young Life staff people who directed the program in our city. We became part of a group of concerned adults who helped give direction to this effective work with teenagers. In our support role, we often took students to weekend or weeklong camps. Camp offered them time away to think about the important matters of their lives.

Some young people came from desperate situations. Their homes were volatile or dangerous. They were making destructive choices. They were considering suicide. Iral and I had a desire to see these kids find meaning in their lives, which led to involvements we had not envisioned. We took time to understand their needs and on several occasions invited them into our family. We never knew if they would stay for a few days or months or years. Our whole family was discovering how to love others in the natural setting of everyday life. Without knowing it we were learning to do what Mother Teresa advised: "Do small things with great love." Even today, all our children are intentional about inviting guests into their families and caring for them.

I would never have described myself as intentional. We just found that once we said goodbye to someone, another opportunity seemed to come our way. Each experience prepared us for the next, which inevitably was a bit more of a stretch for us. On one occasion, a Rotary exchange student from South Africa was not doing well in her host home, and Rotary officials asked us to take her in. She became important to our family. We stayed connected when she returned home, and she became a lifelong friend. This small step to care about a high school student from South Africa eventually raised our concern for people in many parts of Africa. We have made several trips to the continent and have helped Young Life chapters begin in several African countries where teenagers with little focus are being steered by concerned adults.

On another occasion, after a family trip to Germany was hampered by our inability to speak any language but English, I vowed that we would give our grandchildren the gift of language for our rapidly shrinking world. This decision led to bringing Japanese instructors into our home, traveling to Japan with our grandchildren and eventually helping students in Japan. And to think that all I wanted to do was prepare our grandchildren for life in a global society!

A dozen years ago we became aware that the Young Life camps available to Oregon students were overcrowded, and students were being turned away. A group of us met in my living room and became convinced that we should act to meet this need. We began looking for a camp, making several searches though central and eastern Oregon for a place that could be turned into a first-class camp for teenagers.

Twenty years earlier, Baghwan Shree Rajneesh and his cult members moved onto the Big Muddy Ranch near Antelope, Oregon. Brainwashed cult members attempted murders, planned bio-terrorism and ran for public office in an effort to take control of the city and county governments. They left under federal indictment several years later, and the property sat vacant for 10 years. Some friends suggested that we consider the Muddy Ranch for a camp location, but its history, immense size (64,000 acres) and the uncertainty of how to proceed deterred us.

One day my walking group found ourselves within a few miles of the property and decided to take a look at it. Ignoring the barred entrance and No Trespassing sign, I entered the property. In an instant, I knew we had found our campground. As we were being chased away by the caretaker, I could already envision the buildings and open land transformed into a Young Life camp. The process of acquiring and renovating the giant facility was long and complicated. But I stayed with it, and today the Washington Family Ranch is one of the nation's premier youth camps. No one could have predicted the scope and vibrancy of the camp during our living room chat a few years earlier.

I can list many people whom Iral and I have launched: our children, the children who were adopted or who lived in our home, children from the community who visited regularly and visitors who came to refocus their lives at our house before facing their challenges. In the end, however, I believe that we are the main ones who have been launched. I can't believe that I once felt stuck at home. It's my favorite place to be, caring for each person who comes through our door and ready for the adventure that person brings our way.

IRS Enforces the Rules of Business

How did Michael come to see an invigorating purpose in insuring people comply with the federal tax code?

By Mr. Michael Fargo

I recently retired from the Internal Revenue Service. When people hear me say this, they often don't know whether to be happy or sad for me. Their faces seem to say, "Oh, Mike, I am so glad you finally get to leave that horrid place. What a terrible way to have spent your working life!" They couldn't be more wrong. My career at the IRS has been wonderful. I have been able to grow as a person, take on creative challenges, make a significant contribution to my community and country, and influence the lives of many people both inside and outside government. What more could I want?

I suppose I would have liked an easier path to finding meaningful work. I first entered the workforce as a high school dropout in Silicon Valley during the 1960s. I was surrounded by rapidly growing companies desperate for workers, regardless of their education. As a short-sighted teenager, I loved having my own money and the sense of freedom it brought.

I eventually finished high school, briefly attended college and spent two years in the Army. But after my discharge, I passed through many jobs in a lot of different places. I ran a teletype machine for Merrill Lynch, formed a painting company with an old friend, immigrated to Australia where I worked for Reuters newswire service, and returned to the States and spent several years on a General Motors assembly line.

During this decade from 1965-75 my work was primarily a means to an end. It put food on the table and kept a roof over my head. It bought me free time to do the things I wanted to do. Work was a necessary evil, and I began to enjoy it less and less. But my situation was far from unbearable. I was young, single and healthy, and I had this vague sense I would eventually find my way to something more meaningful. Why be in a hurry?

My attitude changed when I got married and in 1977 our first child was born. By then, I was earning a good salary as a computer programmer. The work was intellectually challenging and brought me tremendous satisfaction when I saw my programs actually perform the functions they were programmed to do. Yet I hated that job. The hours were long, the coding was lonely, abstract work, and to be honest, I was not as fast as the others. Did I really want to spend the rest of my life being financially comfortable but miserable? Or did I want my work to mean something to me, to contribute to something, to leave something behind?

I opted for the latter option. Looking at the things I loved and the things I thought I was good at, I decided to return to college and get a teaching degree. With my wife's support and the GI bill's financing, I finished college and became a high school English teacher in 1980. It turned out that I did love my subject, and I was a pretty good teacher. Unfortunately, I never got a handle on classroom management. I couldn't believe how much time I had to spend policing instead of teaching – even when I was working at a very affluent school in Palo Alto, California, where several of my students were children of Nobel Prize-winning professors at Stanford University. One day a student who didn't want to participate in the discussion simply stood up and cursed me to my face. I sent her to the principal, who sent her back to the class with a brief note: "Mr. Fargo – deal with it in the classroom." I knew I was in the wrong place.

We decided to move to Oregon and start fresh. Unfortunately, an all-too-familiar pattern re-emerged. Unable to find a teaching job and desperate to provide for my family (we had two children by then), I took a variety of low-paying jobs, moving to three different towns in an attempt to find something better. In late 1981 I was offered a position by the Internal Revenue Service. I had no background in taxation, accounting or anything remotely connected to the IRS. But I had scored well on the civil service exam and was a veteran, which was enough to earn me a position as a Revenue Officer.

So I became a tax collector. I would be responsible for collecting the unpaid taxes of people and businesses that had ignored all earlier collection attempts by mail and telephone. It was an enforcement job that involved levying wages, seizing and selling property, and sometimes pursuing criminal referrals. The bookish and withdrawn English teacher who had trouble controlling his class had just become a field agent for the U.S. government, complete with a badge, a stack of cases and an awesome amount of authority to get the job done. It was a whole different universe but one that finally brought meaning to my world of work.

I suddenly found myself with more leverage than I ever thought possible, but I also discovered that such leverage requires tremendous responsibility. I was saddled with the job of both protecting the government's interest and helping individuals and companies sort through horrific financial dilemmas. My decisions would greatly impact many people's lives.

Surprisingly, I was good at it. I *cared* about my clients. Even though most feared (and loathed) the IRS, my concern for their problem would usually disarm them enough to build a level of trust that allowed us to work out a reasonable solution. I was developing an ability to help people stay in business, keep their jobs and do the right thing when it came to paying their taxes. I wasn't always successful, but it happened often enough to keep me hopeful for others. My job was now more than a paycheck or an ego stroke. My job had the potential to help people and communities.

There were, of course, a small percentage of people who worked very hard at avoiding their taxes. They would try to hide their income and assets through a myriad of schemes – bogus trusts, inflated expenses, false financial statements and so forth. These clients pursued a cat-and-mouse game unaware that I was a patient, stealthy pursuer. In a different sort of way, I also cared about these people. I was determined to make them do the right thing and ensure and equitable system for the vast majority of people who were paying their fair share of tax. I had to chase one individual through more than 100 partnerships before I was able to corner him through the courts. In the end he paid every dime, and we parted without rancor.

Thomas Jefferson once said that a nation that cannot collect its own revenue will soon cease to exist. My job was showing me that tax collecting not only strengthened communities, but also benefited the tax evaders who reconciled their bills. I could drive down Main Street and see businesses that still existed because I was able to help them overcome their financial difficulties. I could also see the taxes they paid flow back into the community in the form of building projects, unemployment insurance and medical benefits to the elderly.

As the years rolled on I took on more responsibility, becoming a manager and then a national analyst. I wrote a proposal for how the IRS could improve its efficiency and save money, which was eventually adopted. I mentored other employees, helped them get promoted and then watched them flourish at their own jobs. The intangible benefits of my job just kept growing and growing.

As I anticipated retirement, I suspected that the things I learned at the IRS could have been learned at any of my previous jobs. I just wasn't teachable at the time. By the time the IRS offer came, I was desperate for steady work that would allow my family literally to settle down. Determined to make the job work out, I took it on with greater seriousness than ever before. With my teachable attitude, I was able to learn much and to help a lot of people along the way.

Mark of a "Hidden Treasure" Company – Section IV

About People - First Example

What does it mean that business is ultimately all about people? Clearly, a business exists to produce products and services to meet the needs of customers – its focus is people. To be successful, the business relies on the work of its leaders, managers and employees – people. The production of the products and services requires suppliers – people. The net profit the company generates goes partly to provide a fair return to the investors – people. The company carries out its responsibilities (including paying taxes) to the communities in which it operates – people.

Johnson & Johnson Credo

A terrific example of a company that understands, codifies and institutionalized this commitment to serve people is Johnson & Johnson, the multinational manufacturer of health and body care products – Johnson's baby products, Tylenol, Motrin, Zyrtec, Band-Aids, Neutrogena, to name just a few. The original Johnson & Johnson credo was written in 1943 by then-chairman R.W. Johnson Jr., and although the credo has been revised, it remains largely unchanged today (see the accompanying box for the original credo). It masterfully summarizes the company's priorities and provides the guiding principles for employees to follow in the ordinary course of their work.

When writing this manuscript, I called the main telephone number of the Johnson & Johnson headquarters in New Brunswick, N.J. I wanted to talk with the executive assistant to the vice president of human resources to verify that the company still uses the credo. To my surprise, the woman answering the main telephone number was able to answer all my questions. She assured me that the credo was still used. When I asked her what she knew about the credo, she instantly replied, "It reminds us that we all have to be part of making higher quality products at lower costs for our customers." How many receptionists know their company's vision statement and can paraphrase it so clearly?

James C. Collins and Jerry I. Porras in their book *Built to Last*[9] discuss the history and impact the credo has had on the business success of Johnson & Johnson. They note how the management of the company inculcated the credo into the culture of the organization and translated the credo into an organizational structure and into action. Their analysis shows that the credo reflects a culture and a way of viewing the business that has led Johnson & Johnson to consistently be an industry leader over several decades.

Let's take a closer look at what the credo says and means.

- **People Priorities** – Notice the credo is a set of priorities about five groups of people, starting with 1) customers and distributors and moving downward to 2) employees and supervisors, 3) management and executives, 4) members of the communities where the employees live and finally 5) investors. The priority ranking guides the decision process and makes it possible for everyone in the company to understand how decisions are made. All groups must be considered – the company must consistently make a profit for its investors if it is to remain healthy – but not all groups are given equal weight. If each category were of equal importance, decision making becomes very difficult since nothing is more important than something else. When the top priority in decision making is wrong, all subsequent priorities are out of order and result in a string of decisions that constantly need fixing. Johnson & Johnson's success over the past 120 years shows that it has properly ordered its priorities.

- **Commitments** – In addition to ranking each group of people, the credo specifies the company's commitment to each of them. For example, the commitment to the customer includes the delivery of high-quality products at lower prices. Distributors are promised orders that are filled quickly and accurately and bring a fair profit. The descriptions are very concrete and easily understood. They avoid abstract concepts such as "industry-leading products" and "best in breed," which employees would find difficult to visualize and translate into terms that guide them in their daily work. Workers understand what it means to fill orders promptly and accurately for customers. This concrete

---

[9] James C. Collins and Jerry I Porras, *Built to Last,* (HarperCollins, New York City, 1994), pp. 58-61.

wording makes it easy for employees to know how they are contributing to the corporate goals.

- **View of success** – The wording also helps employees determine if they are doing their job with excellence. Supervisors are tasked with providing their workers respect, good working conditions, fair wages and the chance for advancement. Management pledges to work to improve the community. Success in the Johnson & Johnson credo is defined not with numerical metrics alone but by the benefits realized by each group of people. Even the importance of making a profit is seen in light of its value to investors.

- **Causes of success** – Another way to look at all the commitments is from the perspective of causal factors. All of the commitments listed in the credo cause business success. None of them measures success. The credo is not a statement of the metrics that measure business success, but states how people operate. With concrete wording, as I mentioned previously, each group can see how it is expected to add value to the success of the enterprise.

- **What can be controlled** – The credo contains only actions over which the company has control – production, distribution, ethical management, good stewardship. It does not talk about success in terms of comparisons to other companies but rather to internal, controllable standards. Each employee and management person is given actions to take. The credo emphasizes responsibilities over which employees have control.

- **Values** – The credo either states or clearly implies a set of values by which people will operate. For example, the line "Employees must feel free to make suggestions and complaints" implies a respectful environment where each person's suggestions and complaints will receive a thoughtful response. Just and fair treatment of people shows up in several places: "Compensation must be fair and adequate" and "Stockholders should realize a fair return." Ripping people off is not part of the credo. Other values stem from the priorities. Employees have higher value than investors even though investors are very important to the company and must be treated appropriately.

Our Credo
Johnson & Johnson

We believe that our first responsibility is to the doctors, nurses, hospitals,
Mothers, and all others who use our products.
Our products must always be of the highest quality.
We must constantly strive to reduce the cost of these products.
Our orders must be promptly and accurately filled.
Our dealers must make a fair profit.

Our second responsibility is to those who work with us--
The men and women in our plants and offices.
They must have a sense of security in their jobs.
Wages must be fair and adequate,
Management just, hours reasonable, and working conditions clean and orderly.
Employees should have an organized system for suggestions and complaints.
Supervisors and department heads must be qualified and fair-minded.
There must be opportunity for advancement for those qualified
And each person must be considered an individual,
Standing on his own dignity and merit.

Our third responsibility is to our management.
Our executives must be persons of talent, education, experience, and ability.
They must be persons of common sense and full understanding.

Our fourth responsibility is to the communities in which we live.
We must be a good citizen--support good works and charity,
And bear our fair share of taxes.
We must maintain in good order the property we are privileged to use.
We must participate in promotion of civic improvement,
Health, education and good government,
And acquaint the community with our activities.

Our fifth and last responsibility is to our stockholders.
Business must make a sound profit.
Reserves must be created, research must be carried on,
Adventurous programs developed, and mistakes paid for.
Adverse times must be provided for, adequate taxes paid, new machines purchased,
New plants built, new products launched, and new sales plans developed.
We must experiment with new ideas.
When these things have been done, the stockholder should receive a fair return.
We are determined with the help of god's grace,
To fulfill these obligations to the best of our ability.

This is the text of the original 1943 Credo as penned by R.W. Johnson, Jr.

- **What the credo is not** – Looking at what the credo does not say becomes equally instructive. As I already mentioned, the credo does not make any statements about how the company stacks up with any of its competitors. It has no statement of market share or rate of company growth, no statement about being an industry leader, no statement of industry leading products and no statement about the quality, capabilities or expertise of any employees except for executives. Obviously, all of these are important, but they are outcomes realized when the credo's actions are carried out.

The Johnson & Johnson credo is neither a vision statement nor mission statement as we normally see them today in corporate America. Rather, it is a comprehensive statement of standards that applies to all employees. Each employee can easily understand his or her everyday work in one of the five responsibilities.

The real world

No doubt many present and former Johnson & Johnson employees can relate stories of how some executive, manager or employee violated the credo. I'm sure there are countless times when people working at Johnson & Johnson do not follow the credo when making their judgments. The purpose of this chapter is not to make a case that employees of Johnson & Johnson live in an organization that is free of the usual inequities caused by inappropriate judgments and decisions by other employees, but rather to show that it is possible for a company to be highly successful when it views itself through the lens of interacting with and caring for people.

The bottom line of the Johnson & Johnson credo is that it drives the company's success by providing employees with a compass to guide their work and decisions. Numerous MBA case studies document critical decisions that have affected Johnson & Johnson's business success. Many of these studies cite the importance of the credo in guiding the decision-making process, especially when executives have little time or information in which to make their decisions. One such famous decision was to pull Tylenol off the shelves in 1982 when reports emerged linking Tylenol to the mysterious deaths of seven people in the Chicago area. The company conducted a countrywide recall of its product at the cost of hundreds of millions of dollars. The case studies show how the credo helped executives make decisions before all the information was available. They even considered the last priority of providing a fair return to stockholders. When the company reintroduced Tylenol capsules to the market, they came in tamper-resistant packaging. The multiple decisions that resulted in safeguarding the public's health were a major factor in maintaining the trust that people had in Johnson & Johnson products.

The Johnson & Johnson credo is a fantastic explanation of how business is all about people. That framework has been a key factor in creating a company that many consider to be the industry leader. Johnson & Johnson proves beyond any shadow of doubt that industry leading companies can base their success on inculcating into their culture the value that business is all about people – customers, employees, suppliers, and investors. We can trust that the framework can be the bedrock for highly effective and successful organizations.

Bringing Structure to People's Dreams

Dick consistently brought value to his clients. But it wasn't until a client made an off-handed comment that his purpose jumped out at him.

By Mr. Dick Sawdey

I've been an attorney for 40 years, half of them in private practice. For the first 30+ years of my career, I provided services to my clients. For the past few, I've provided "structure to people's dreams". Far from a catchy marketing slogan, the "word shift" has helped me understand what motivates me to do the legal work I do. I need to know I'm doing more than simply supplying competent legal advice.

In the early years, I didn't consider the lofty questions of dreams and purpose. I entered law school directly after graduating college because of the wide variety of career options that appealed to me. Years earlier my mother had remarked that my ability to read and comprehend would be good skills for a lawyer to have. She was right. I loved my classes, the emphasis on analysis and reasoning and the feeling that I knew how the system worked. I was confident I would make a good attorney.

If only I had some idea of what type of law I wanted to practice. I had had almost no direct contact with an attorney in private practice. By the time I graduated, I was married and expecting our first child. Earning a living became my immediate priority. Since the best jobs for new lawyers were in big cities, I was attracted to the one nearest me – Chicago. I landed a job with a mid-sized firm, where I gained a solid foundation, but after a few years became impatient and somewhat bored. My attitude distressed me. Wasn't I doing the work I wanted? Hadn't I prepared for this for many years? Ultimately, I left the firm after five years, my restlessness caused by the repetitive nature of my job. I was much more attracted to learning a task than repeating it 50 times.

My next job – at a large corporation that offered a greater variety of tasks – kept my interest for 15 years, but it too lost its luster. Although I had been promoted to vice president and the firm's corporate secretary, I began to feel that I was coasting, that I needed a greater professional and personal challenge. Once again, my attitude distressed me. I had striven hard to get where I was. My position and the company were terrific. I was too old to think about a new career. People my age were supposed to be settled in their life's work.

I started another job search. I asked a friend in the executive search business to have lunch with me. I told him that I wanted his advice on my resume, but I was secretly hoping that he might know of a position for me and my quest would be over before it had begun. My friend had a very different agenda. He wanted to know about my first law firm job. What had I enjoyed the most? He lit up when I told him that the most fulfilling times were when I had the opportunity to represent my own clients, people who had come to me for advice as opposed to persons who were clients of other attorneys in the firm.

I could see where the conversation was leading, and I didn't like it at all. It was ridiculous to consider opening my own practice. I'd been practicing corporate law for 15 years; I didn't have a single client. I had never managed a law practice or been in business for myself. I had a family, kids in college. I wasn't interested in starting over. I left the lunch irritated that he hadn't helped me like I wanted.

But my friend had accomplished his goal. The idea he had planted now haunted me. I couldn't get the vision of own law practice out of my mind. In idle moments, I imagined myself doing it. No matter how hard I tried to shove it down, it kept rising up.

I decided to at least investigate the idea. I met with several lawyers who had made significant job changes in mid-life. Each had gone through struggles. None had any regrets. I now had no excuses. If they could do it, I could do it. The big issue was money. Was I willing to give up my salary and benefits for zero compensation? My wife helped me see that I could. Her teaching salary would buy our food and pay the mortgage, and we had the resources saved to finance the balance of our kids' college educations. My family would be fine. But could I risk being a total failure? Yes, I could live with that possibility.

I found a firm willing to give me a position known as "of counsel" where I would have all the services provided to any attorney in the firm – an office, secretarial support, a key to the men's room – with one big exception: no salary. As I developed clients, I gave them a portion of the fees I collected. I immediately got to work developing those clients.

It turned out to be the perfect move for me. I was free to find creative solutions to problems I had never encountered before instead of being enslaved by a high number of repetitive tasks. After 10 years, I was invited to become a partner in the firm. I expected to finally feel settled. Instead, I felt my uneasiness coming back, this time at a more fundamental level: What was it that I really did for my clients? Was there any unique contribution that I could provide? In essence, I was questioning my real purpose.

The answer came from a non-profit client who was thankful for all the contingencies I had addressed for their organization. It was quite a feat to have all the parties involved come away feeling results would be fair should events and people follow unexpected paths. Having a structure that can encompass a variety of contingencies, they told me, was a major step to realizing their dreams.

It was an interesting idea: I brought structure to people's dreams. It made sense for the non-profit group. The client has a dream to make a positive change in the world, and I set up the structure – the tax-exempt organization – for achieving the dream. As I thought it through, I could see how this concept applied to all my clients in all aspects of legal issues. Estate planning clients have dreams (although they commonly call them goals or objectives). They want to see their hard-earned family assets transmitted to their children or charities in a responsible and creative manner. The right structure will insure their objectives are achieved without confusion or family feuding.

Likewise, business clients have dreams (they too call them goals) for a successful enterprise. They are likely investing a high level of energy and financial resources and carrying a high level of risk. They value an advisor who understands their unique goals and can structure the business documents to help them get what they want. Business agreements and contracts that include well-considered contingencies maximize harmonious business transactions and minimize acrimonious dealings and lawsuits.

Having only recently discovered this truth, I feel like the author of a book who finished the manuscript and then had the title magically jump off the page. It could not have been known any earlier. Certainly at the outset of my career, I was not thinking in terms of bringing structure to people's dreams. I was thinking simply of servicing clients. If someone wanted X, I gave them X. Having the idea of dream fulfillment jump out at me has brought a sense of unity to my career overall.

I see how all along my way, I was guided, sometimes in very small ways, along the path necessary to get me to where I am today. A remark from my mother, an interview in Chicago, a chance encounter with a friend, an uncomfortable lunch, an off-hand comment; each led me to act – to ask questions, explore new opportunities, talk to a friend – and to wait for a defining moment that offered me the opportunity to say yes to something new. My latest "yes" is to the fun I experience as I bring people the creative structure that turns their dreams into reality.

From Family Development to Business Development

Dianne enjoyed spending full-time with her daughters as they grew up. To her surprise that prepared her for developing businesses.

By Ms. Dianne Doherty

Most people my age are winding down in their careers, but mine seems to be going full tilt. Perhaps because I got a late start, I now find my work so meaningful. Plus I'm having a lot of fun.

After earning a philosophy degree from Mount Holyoke College in 1959, I spent one year in the workforce before staying home to raise my family. I watched my four daughters grow and maintained my sanity through volunteer work. Twenty years later, my girls were practically grown and I knew I had to do more than live life vicariously through my husband, Paul. I was ready to return to the workforce.

Although my years of volunteering had taught me a lot about management, leadership and organizational development, they weren't very marketable to the business world. Neither was my philosophy degree. I was compelled to go back to school, an intimidating proposition. The other students (not to mention many professors) were half my age. I had to master statistics. But once I got over the discomfort and believed that I could succeed, I began to love the academic setting and its encouraging and supportive environment.

I earned my MBA in 1981 and went to work at an adverting agency where a good friend was a partner. After sitting in on one new business presentation and armed with one item from the company's portfolio, I tried to land new accounts. I made my way with on-the-job training and was glad when I was offered a position to run a marketing campaign for the city of Springfield, MA, and some major business sponsors.

When the two-year funding decreased, I was forced to find a new position. A colleague and I decided to start a marketing company – we had one client with which to pave the way. We slowly added more, from mom-and-pop shops to Fortune 100 companies, each one presenting a wide variety of (often daunting) challenges. When our largest client, a local bank, decreased its annual advertising budget from $800,000 to $50,000, daunting became discouraging.

I next landed at the Small Business Development Center, part of the Isenberg School of Management at the University of Massachusetts Amherst. I initially intended to spend two or three years providing business advisory services and management training programs to entrepreneurs. Eighteen years later, I am still there and I still love it.

Working with entrepreneurs is extremely rewarding. Energy, creativity, intelligence, ambition, drive and determination are indigenous to the species. Their effectiveness rides on these factors. They are challenged by my probing questions that sharpen their focus and clarify their action steps as a result. It is motivating to be included in their journeys. I can offer my real-world experience, the analytical skills I developed at business school, my experience in raising our four daughters and even my abiding interest in philosophy's great questions – What constitutes a meaningful life? In what ways does work enhance or degrade our deepest purpose on earth? Such questions help people articulate the value they bring to customers and employees alike. Knowing that I can parlay my business and life experience for the benefit of others has been a road to establishing my self-worth and purpose.

I serve on the board of Digital Divide Data (www.digitaldividedata.org), a social venture that provides job training, English and computer skills to disabled and disadvantaged youth in Cambodia and Laos. The lack of good leadership and managerial talent in those countries stands in sharp contrast to opportunities available in the United States. My long association with highly creative entrepreneurs certainly validates what as Carl Schramm so eloquently and persuasively stated in *The Entrepreneurial Imperative*,[10] that entrepreneurship is one of our best exports and can be the base for spreading peace and democracy throughout the world.

My career has been inspired by Martin Luther King's view that "no work is insignificant. All labor that uplifts humanity has dignity and

---

[10] Carl J. Schramm, Ph.D., *The Entrepreneurial Imperative: How America's Economic Miracle Will Reshape the World (and Change Your Life),* (Harper Collins, New York, 2006)

importance and should be undertaken with painstaking excellence." While I have generally worked diligently at whatever I undertake, I have also had fun (and been challenged and humbled). The small business owners I advise each bring their own degree of ability, facility, confidence, curiosity, energy, resourcefulness and passion to their companies. I want to affirm these talents and give them the tools to succeed in establishing businesses that can in turn uplift those that they encounter. Being part of this is a noble pursuit as well as just plain energizing and meaningful.

Mark of a "Hidden Treasure" Leader – Section V

People-Focused Leadership

As we've already discussed and seen in several examples, an ultimate purpose of work is to invest in others. Workers show their care externally through the products and services they provide people. In this chapter, we will look at the internal workings of a company. When a company is all about people, how do its managers and executives operate? With what context or framework should they define success? Will a focus on people lead to highly effective leaders and managers? Is such a framework realistic?

Rookie managers struggle to "see" their management responsibilities in the appropriate framework. They want to please both their bosses and those they now supervise – they have to ensure that their team gets all its tasks done yet still treat their people fairly. When I was first promoted into management, I enrolled in a series of courses that taught me a wide array of techniques for helping others do their job with excellence and for preventing me from micromanaging or meddling in their work. The techniques, however, always boiled down to the same thing: manipulating people into making sure they accomplished the work I needed done and insuring they did it on time and within budget. I was like a carpenter using a hammer. People were my tools – they would hang from my tool belt until I needed them, and they would get used until I was done with them.

Even though I was young and inexperienced, I could see that mastering these techniques would get all the group's work accomplished but would also leave me with angry workers. Who likes to be manipulated or treated like a tool in a toolbox? How long would a resentful team sustain a high level of excellence and creativity? I was stuck in this huge dilemma: how to get my team to produce the required deliverables on schedule without using and abusing them through the process. I wanted a better way.

Redefining a manager's role

Several years after becoming a manager, I happened to be meeting with the late Ray Regimbal, who was a vice chairman of Johnson & Johnson at the time. After the meeting I told him of my dilemma. Without hesitation, he told me, "The purpose of a manager is to be responsible to his or her direct reports for their development." It took me a minute to really hear what he was saying. Here was the person in charge of all of Europe and Africa for Johnson & Johnson telling me, not that management was about business development, but that it focused on the development of each individual. If I had not known this man's accomplishments and his reputation as a very successful and hard-nosed businessman dealing with fierce market competition, I would have dismissed his comment as that of a do-gooder. I would expect his quote to come from a social worker or school teacher but not from a pragmatic, realistic business executive. I was dumbfounded. Not knowing what to say, I just stood there like a post.

> *"The purpose of a manager is to be responsible to his or her direct reports for their development."*

I have thought about the ramifications of his statement for a long time. Not only did he challenge me to put people first, but I was impressed with how he told me to do it. Look at his prepositions. He did not say the manager is responsible *for* a person's development but *to* a person *for* them to take responsibility for their own development. If the person chooses not to develop, that forces certain responses from the manager and limits the opportunities for the person. This correspondingly limits what the manager can do for that person. I have worked with people who would have been great at bringing out the latent skills of younger workers yet chose to work alone rather than have the joys and complexities of working closely with others. These senior people missed out on developing their latent skills to pass on the secrets they knew.

Over the next several years I kept working at understanding all the wisdom contained in Regimbal's words. It became my defining mindset for managing people. I began to explain to people not only the business payoff of their assignment but also how the personal growth in capability they desired got developed along the way. I was able to help them see that the success of the company provided the environment to grow as people. This was especially helpful to them when they had to do something in which they saw no personal benefit.

Fundamentally, the quote puts work and the people at work in a much larger context where they are synergistic rather than competing. Development of people brings benefits far beyond the work environment. After all, people use their competency and experience wherever they are – whether at work, home or even spending time with friends. This larger context helps me understand how work integrates with the rest of our lives.

Through absorbing and assimilating Regimbal's short quote, I learned that it contains a number of key concepts about business and my role in it. They're listed below and detailed in the paragraphs that follow.

- Business success is the constraint of the game, not the purpose of work.
- A manager's commitment to people increases his or her commitment to the business's success.
- The direct report has to be committed to doing all of his or her job for the manager to be able to develop the person.
- The manager deals with "what" needs to be done, the staff with "how" it gets done.
- The manager has both public and private goals.
- The manager uses the company to build people rather than people to build the company.

Business success is the constraint, not the purpose.

My whole understanding begins by putting business success in the proper perspective. Even though the manager is committed to the business's success, he or she understands that this commitment is not his or her purpose. The purpose is the development of staff. Business success is the constraint of the game, the structure that defines how everyone operates – no business, no game. This perspective leads to the great management paradox: Managers who focus on the development of people within the constraints of the success of the business contribute more to the success of the business. As I cared more about staff development and less about the success of the business, I was very surprised to actually find myself more committed to the business's success. If you're like me, that idea will take a good deal of thought to get straight in your mind: care less; commit more. That leads to the next concept, in which we will explore the paradox a bit more.

Manager is intensely committed to business success.

In order to focus on the development of staff, there has to be staff. In order for there to be staff, there has to be a successful business that needs staff. Thus, if a manager is seriously committed to being responsible to his or her direct reports for their development, the manager has to be committed to doing *all* of his or her job. In the process, the manager develops an intense commitment to the business's success. In fact, it is very likely that a manager with a clear commitment to the development of staff will have a much deeper commitment to the success of the business than a person who does not concentrate on staff development.

The commitment to doing all of the manager's job shows up in being extra-ordinary – doing his or her ordinary tasks with excellence. That means knowing what needs to be done, having the competency needed to do it and persisting at it relentlessly. The manager with such a commitment often has much more enjoyment while executing these responsibilities. A credo like Johnson & Johnson's, as detailed in Section IV, becomes a great guide for these daily tasks.

More fundamentally, a manager who is committed to business success because of a commitment to direct reports cares about the business for the right reason. The manager is much less likely to have selfish motivations such as getting a promotion, protecting his or her job, taking credit for results and/or creating an outstanding personal and professional reputation. Because the manager genuinely cares about others, the manager ends up making a clearing in which others can flourish. He or she ends up building highly effective teams. These are all results of setting the right priorities.

The great management paradox of caring more about people than the business has its roots in the fact that the development of people results in a better company than does the manipulation of people. People know when they are being manipulated, and they quickly learn to resent the manipulator. The more manipulation, the greater the resentment. Conversely, when people are developed, they are in a position to be invigorated and gain more skills to accomplish the tasks that build the company. For example, a person with sub-par communication skills can be enrolled in a writing course. The resulting ability to write clear reports and make effective presentations adds value to both the business and the employee's skill set.

The bottom line? Developing people to have capability X ends up getting task Y accomplished, which often results in increased revenue or decreased costs – either makes the company more successful.

Direct reports commit to doing all of their job.

A manager's commitment to the personal development of his or her direct reports is only half of the equation. The direct reports must commit to doing all of the job assigned to them. They must be willing to put in a full day's work for a full day's pay. If they don't make that commitment, the manager's hands are tied when it comes to their development. Instead of being able to focus on developing direct reports, the manager has to focus on getting them to sign up for what they are being paid to do. The manager is very restricted in developing a person under this circumstance. Thus, a key prerequisite for a manager is having people who are committed to doing their job. Fortunately, most people desire to do a job well. Even so, management usually has to provide some reminders and some encouragement when a person has to plow through the mundane tasks and discouragement that all work seems to have.

Of course, if direct reports do not want to be developed, the manager cannot force them. The manager can do little but watch to see if they become dissatisfied because of the lack of growth. If that occurs, the manager decides if it is best for a person to move to a new position or even on to another company. A manager might also recommend an individual change organizations if the current one does not offer the right type of development opportunities and would cause the individual to stagnate.

Manager's and staff's roles are clear.

With managers committed to staff development and the staff being developed into who they can be, a common question might arise: Is anybody getting any work done? In my mind, an employee's daily tasks – the work – are a given. They are the constraints of the job. Before people are hired, they agree to these constraints and that they will come to work to do them – fill up customers' gas tanks, bus tables, prosecute criminals, run the company, hit home runs.

The constraints are ***what*** needs to get done, and the people committed to the constraints determine ***how*** they get done. The manager is responsible to define "what" has to get done to accomplish the goals of the company and then create an environment in which the direct reports have the tools, resources and authority to figure out "how" each task is accomplished. I find that the annoying micro-manager meddles in "how" the job gets done, the unclear manager fails to clearly define "what" needs to be done, and neither knows the line of demarcation between the two. For effective teamwork, it is imperative that the manager keeps to the "what" and the direct report sticks to the "how."

Managers have many tools for developing their staff. Three of them include:

1. The creation of a healthy environment for learning and improving skills
2. The distribution of tasks among the people in the group to maximize each person's development
3. The implementation and support of ongoing classes for education and training

Manager has public and private purposes.[11]

Everybody is driven by a set of core values and beliefs. In almost all cases, it is best for effective managers to keep these inner motivations to themselves. That way they are not weighed down by the expectations others would heap upon them. Instead managers communicate a public objective to their direct reports and boss, while their private purpose quietly guides their management decisions. It is not that the private and public contradict each other. Generally, the public purpose provides the business context in which the private purpose safely operates and allows managers to be evaluated by what they do, not by what they say they believe.

The following table shows an example of two public purposes alongside the private purposes of both a development-oriented manager and a manipulative manager.

---

[11] Brian Baugh, my son, conceived and documented this useful concept of the public and private purposes of a manager as a result of one of our family discussions.

Manager's Purpose		
Public	**Private**	
	Development Manager	**Manipulative Manager**
Build business so that I have more opportunities to develop people.	Discover greater purpose for my work in order to have passion, drive and significance at work.	Build business and help it succeed so that I look good.
Serve direct reports to enable them to better execute their tasks.	Develop the direct reports into who their talents allow them to be.	Manipulate direct reports so that I look good.

Manager uses the company to build people.

Ultimately a manager has to choose between using the company to build people or using people to build the company. The management paradox, as I stated earlier, is that choosing to use the company to fully develop people in their work environment ends up building the company.

A manager's motives are the key to this paradox. Managers cannot truly develop people if deep down their motives are self-serving. Manipulation can masquerade as service and love, but it is a cloak that can sabotage the development of a direct report and, consequently, hurt the business. Direct reports are very good at detecting a boss's true motives. This is why it is so important for managers to control their self-interests and continually examine their motives. It's not always easy to follow this higher purpose, but it's the truest way for managers to meet their business responsibilities while helping their direct reports to flourish.

The following table shows the manager's motives undergirding the purposes shown in the prior table.

Noble goals are not always indicators of pure motives. A manager can have the worthy goal of feeding starving people, but the motive might be to build up the manager's image to look like a great altruist. If that's the case, I would contend that the manager's real purpose is self-serving – to build up his or her image – and he or she is likely to manipulate direct reports to accomplish this goal.

Manager's Motive		
Public	**Private**	
	Development Manager	**Manipulative Manager**
Be responsible:	Love:	Look out for me:
Execute my responsibilities with excellence and produce the deliverables assigned to me and my group or organization.	Develop direct reports while they each produce the deliverables assigned to them.	Do what it takes to obtain position, power, promotions, prestige, notoriety, approval of boss, respect, titles, money, etc.

In the end, managers will either pursue prestige, power, position, advancement and security or will pursue love and service. Unless the motives are to serve others instead of serving the self, managers will not able to accomplish their true private purpose. If they care more for their own payoffs, they will end up using their direct reports for their own selfish gain. They will be creating resentment instead of developing people.

Of course, no one is perfect and able to have pure motivations all of the time, but an awareness of motives will solve many problems in leadership and management. Serving others ahead of one's self will lead to effective management and therefore successful businesses. Ultimately, and here's another paradox, those who serve others end up benefiting themselves as well. It's just hard to believe this and have our whole being lined up to act as if this is so.

Ray Regimbal's wisdom has saved me untold amounts of grief. It always works. And when I fail to heed it, I discover anew the ramifications of putting my selfish gain or business success above the development of people.

An example of how not to manage staff

Let's look at an example of how not to relate to employees. This comes from the teacher performance review form from a suburban Seattle school district for the 2000-2001 school year. The form contains the following statement:

The purpose of this [performance] evaluation is to: enhance the total learning environment for students and the general improvement of instruction.

While the purpose sounds noble – Who wouldn't want their children's learning environment enhanced? – this evaluation form overlooks the primary purpose of school administrators: to develop their teachers. This simple sentence sends a message that the district is not interested in the teacher for anything other than the teacher's ability to enhance the total learning environment. Teachers are not valued as individuals but for the role they fill. They are a means to an end, being used just like the computers and textbooks to fulfill classroom tasks. Most likely, the administrators would disagree with this assessment, but I contend that the words on the form focus on business success that indicates a utilitarian view of teachers and fosters an environment of resentment and low morale.

So how would the performance evaluation read if the administration had a larger view of teacher development and the contributions that teachers make? It would say something like:

The purpose of this performance evaluation is: to develop you as the best teacher you can be, given that the school has been entrusted with the public responsibility to enhancing the total learning environment for students and the general improvement of instruction.

The administrator's purpose now becomes teacher development, not learning environment enhancement. Enhancing the environment is very important, but it must be put in its proper place: as the constraint or byproduct of all the people in the organization doing their jobs. The primary purpose focuses on the development of the individual teacher, not the task that has to be accomplished by all the teachers with the support, resources and leadership of the administration. The focus is on the cause of the result, not the result itself. The administration commits to the incredible value of the employee within the constraint or context of the responsibility entrusted to the organization by its customers and other stakeholders.

The administration focuses on the development of its teachers, and the teachers focus on the development of their students. When administrators provide the tools and create the environment for the success of the teacher and teachers assume their commitments, the byproduct of a quality learning environment naturally occurs. The administrators tackle the "what" of education: They determine the objectives that teachers have to accomplish and provide the development opportunities that help them accomplish those goals. Then the teachers determine the "how:" They, not the administrators, focus on how they are to teach the material to their students.

As long as the teacher is committed to becoming the best teacher he or she can be, the administration is free to be excited about the growth of the teacher and the resulting improvements in instruction as well as other positive impacts on society. Could administrators take the same actions to improve the teachers' abilities to teach even when development is not their primary purpose? Of course. The message the teachers receive from the administration, however, will be very different depending on the focus – I am being used versus I am being valued.

Of course, if a teacher is not meeting the requirements of the task of teaching, then the teacher cannot be allowed to continue in the job. It is not love to continue to let people fail because they are trying to do something for which they are not competent or do not have the basic talents, skills, interests and motivations needed to succeed. But if the teacher cares about the students and has the requisite talent and skills, he or she would commit to personal development that results in enhancing the learning environment and improving instruction.

What if the organization does not succeed?

A manager can operate with a people focus even when the company does not succeed. My career testifies to this. The first company I joined had more than a million employees. Just after I left, the government forced it to break up into several companies. The subsidiary with which I worked is but a shadow of its former self and very different from what it was.

The next company with which I worked acted as the cash cow for starting a cellular telephone company in the United Kingdom. That company has become the largest mobile phone operator in the world. Management made a brilliant business decision to take our profits to start a new company. But it caused the company with which I worked to starve to death.

The next company I joined wanted to do a startup within its very large manufacturing company. After finally understanding what the business was all about, management pulled the plug on the startup and put me in a position that was a huge mismatch for my interests and skills.

I left to join another company that was later consolidated back to its headquarters in another state. I was laid off. That led to a sequence of unpredictable, but fortuitous, circumstances that launched my consulting business.

Other than my consulting business, none of the companies for which I worked ended up being successful in the long run. During my years at each, however, I became increasingly more people focused in both my management view and my business commitments. By the time I became a consultant; Ray Regimbal's mindset was ingrained in me and helped me develop my own successful business.

Summary

Ray Regimbal's mindset – "the purpose of a manager is to be responsible to his or her direct reports for their development" – provides a way not only to care about people, but also to care even more about the business being successful. In a very real but subtle way, a person cares less about the business's success but actually commits even more to it. Regimbal further inverts traditional business thinking when he advocates that, instead of using people to build the company, using the company to care about people – customers, employees, suppliers and investors. As a manager, I use the company to build the people for whom I have responsibility. It has to be done within the constraints of the business – it can only be done if the company continues to succeed. My commitment to people actually enlarges and deepens my commitment to the success of the business.

The quote integrates all the seemingly contradictory demands placed on a manager into a coherent whole where each demand energizes the others. A manager not only gets tasks done with excellence but also provides healthy growth for people. How stimulating is that?

Recognizing the ramifications of Regimbal's quote leads to a manager's priority being first on people and then second on tasks, and proves to be congruent with success on the job. A people focused manager does match up with business reality. The framework of making people more important than tasks within the constraints that the work must get done provides the key to "seeing" how to find the purpose of our work – the hidden treasure in the work we do. Thus, the framework is realistic, matches up with the responsibilities of management and allows us to entrust our career to it. Moreover, the people first perspective benefits both bosses and employees. It is worthy of our trust no matter what role we have in an institution.

Indebtedness to Employees

Little did Bill know that he would have a startling experience that completely changed the landscape on how he invests in his business.

By Mr. Bill Simmons

Over the course of about 15 years, I got fired from every job I had. When I started each new job, the boss was very happy with me and my work. But over time, I started to have difficulty with my supervisor, and our interactions became increasingly acrimonious until my boss decided that my antics were too disruptive and I needed to work somewhere else.

There is one other quirk that I carry around. I have a very low tolerance for poor customer service. The way all customers are treated is very important to me and, much to the embarrassment of my family, I have been known to make a scene and stomp out of a restaurant when the service is less than satisfactory.

A third important fact is that now I'm the business owner. I set the standards for my employees, and I set the standard for customer service.

I had been unemployed for about three years and was three months behind on my mortgage when I finally decided to find a legitimate job. Since I was pretty bad at being the employee, I thought I'd try being the owner instead. I met with a friend who was a local banker and told him I wanted to buy a business that was in trouble but was salvageable. In February 1981, after a few months of negotiations, I signed a deal with the owners of a Minit Lube franchise. I would run the business for a year, and if, at the end of the year, I could afford to make the monthly payments still owed to the franchiser, I would take full ownership. We also worked out a deal with Minit Lube to be released from the franchise contract so I could own the business outright. At the end of the year, I was able to make the monthly payments. I renamed the business MasterLube and still run it today.

As soon as I stepped in to run the lube business, my customer service fixation kicked in. I instituted several new standards. We would greet a customer within six seconds of their turning into our establishment and greet them before they had time to park. No male employee would ever patronize or look down at a woman customer. We would kneel down and be at eye level when talking with a woman driver and treat her as though she were their favorite aunt. We would not just be good at our jobs – we would make sure customers knew that we were good at what we did. I knew that my demanding employee training had paid off when one day a customer spontaneously applauded for the guys doing the work.

Given my work history, I was quite surprised that I really enjoyed my employees, most of whom were high school dropouts. Although they didn't know it – and never even thought to look for it – they all had great talent. After the store closed in the evening, as we cleaned up and set up cases of oil for the next day, we talked. Often we cracked out some beer, and they told me about their lives. Not a single one had high aspirations for their life. Some were very surprised to still be alive.

I didn't share the low opinion they had of themselves. I knew they were helping my business succeed. I never realized their full value, however, until a night in 1982. I woke up in the dead of night with my conscience groaning in agony. I had been assaulted with the awareness of how much my employees added to my business' financial success. I was paying them minimum wage but getting three to five times that much productivity from them. I was incurring a huge debt to my own employees. Every hour and every day they worked, I owed them more.

The realization haunted me. At work that week I examined my books and discovered that I could not have a viable business if I paid my employees at the level they produced. I was in debt to them with no idea how to pay it down. I was desperate for a solution.

I was surprised how quickly the solution came. Maybe it was the result of all the hours I spent talking with my workers or maybe it was because I had once been where they now were, but I saw that these young men and women had so much more potential than they were using, and I wanted to help them discover that potential. I would pay down the debt I owed them by rallying all the resources I had around town to help them become who they could be.

I scheduled lunch with one of the men and explained my dilemma. I told him that I was totally aware of how much he and his co-workers contributed to the success of the business and how their pay did not reflect that contribution. Thus, I was in debt to them. I couldn't pay it off in cash but could pay it in other ways. I explained that I saw skills and talents in him that would take him to a very different job and career, one that would not only pay more but also provide more satisfaction. I was willing to spend time and find resources to assist him to get there. He looked at me like I had two heads and was speaking Japanese. A week later I had another lunch discussion with another young man. It had the same result.

I was discovering that not only were these men and women unaware of their skills and talents, but they lacked the aspirations to live beyond today. They had no idea who they really were and no motivation to find out. My task would be formidable, but I wasn't about to give up. I found the plan I needed in the writings of management consultant Peter Drucker: 1) Discover your core competencies, 2) decide what you want to be when you grow up, and 3) choose a career that can be a tool to reach your goal.

Before I could help them discover their core competencies, they would need to change their self-perceptions. They needed to see that they were not doomed to be victims of life but could make good things happen for themselves. Surprisingly, my customer service fixation helped them learn that truth. They knew that they had control over whether a customer had a positive or negative experience. They determined whether a customer would want to come back. Creating customer satisfaction had the added benefit of raising my employees' self-perception.

Another goal was to help them develop larger aspirations for their lives, to think in terms of leaving a legacy rather than simply surviving another day. Again, it required a change in their perspective. Our after-hours conversations took a new turn. I might ask a guy to picture himself lying critically ill in a hospital bed, tubes coming out of every part of him. I would ask him to reflect on his life. What was it he did that was significant and why? Whom did it affect? Those discussions helped them think a little broader. Sometimes tangible problems emerged, and my management team and I addressed those. If someone had an anger issue, we made it possible for them to get counseling. If someone couldn't manage their money, we provided a means for financial management training. We encouraged them to earn their GEDs.

Once they had an initial grasp of their aspirations, I could talk to them about their appearance and the message it conveyed. Did it welcome people in or drive them away? If the next customer turned out to be a potential future employer, did they sow seeds of opportunity or wash away any hope for a job?

I was focusing my efforts on a couple of the young men, stumbling and fumbling my way through. I realized that the transformation would take time, two to three years, but I was willing to make the investment.

In 1985 – inspired by the "big hairy audacious goal" described in the book *Built to Last*[12] – I challenged our employees with the outrageous goal of developing the best lube business in the country and making sure the world knew it. I wanted all the industry journals to write about us and all the major lube franchises to visit us and learn the secrets of our success. By 1989 we had accomplished our goal. But we didn't slow down. We now have the highest-volume, two-bay store in the country and outperform nearly all the metrics in our industry. We also have three other MasterLube stores, two car washes, and one automobile glass store. People come from outside the county to watch the "show" as well as get their car serviced. My employees now see the great work they do and the great environment they have created.

We are on the fifth iteration of our training program that not only gets the employees to perform on the job but gets them to create their own career. When I hire someone now, I ask them to stick with us for three years. By the end of three years, they will have mastered the job and have no place to grow. The work will no longer engage their creative energy, and they will need to move on to a more challenging career. More than half make it through, and when they do their pictures and stories are added to the Alumni Wall at the store (two alumni stories appear at the end of the chapter).

I could never have predicted this success when I took over the struggling lube business in 1981. My history certainly didn't indicate I'd get these results. But every day I remind myself that all my employees have incredible talent and potential and are bringing more value to me than I can pay, that I am accruing a debt that I have to pay down. I am more committed than ever to providing an environment where they can make major moves toward realizing that potential. It took all the experiences of my previous jobs to give me the empathy, understanding and motivation I needed for living out this deep-seated conviction and passion.

---

[12] James C. Collins and Jerry I Porras, *Built to Last*, pp. 91-114.

At the end of every day I glance at our Alumni Wall and wonder how many more pictures it can hold. I don't want to stop until it's overflowing.

MasterLube Alumni

Robert Hill
Alumni 1994-1996

Fighting is in Robert's blood. But for a quite while, Robert spent more time around blood than he did fighters.

Robert worked here as a technician while pursuing his goal of working in health care and going to school for phlebotomy. After completing his classes, he went to work at a local laboratory as a phlebotomist.

But, as they often do, his goals changed over time and he felt a strong desire to return to the sports his grandfather and father loved. In April 2008, Robert opened 5 Star MMA to teach self-defense, mixed-martial arts, judo, boxing and a variety of other fighting styles. His goals are now focused on his family and his fighters. He proudly speaks of his oldest son's first-degree black belt and the goals he has for each of his students. And we proudly speak of him.

"Enjoy the time you have and get as much as you can out of your work experience."

Joanne Wambeke
Alumni 1980-1986

Joanne has her fair share of job titles, but back in 1980 she had one – Cashier for our store.

Joanne worked for us through high school and while obtaining her degree in business and psychology at Carroll College. While she was a very young employee, she was goal driven, worked hard and had a great attitude.

She later went on to get her master's degree and now owns her own private counseling practice and works with college students on another continent as the Director of Student Affairs for the International College at Beijing through the University of Colorado Denver. She now seeks to help others reach their full potential, and we're proud to see she's reached hers.

"It matters less what you do than how you do it... have high integrity and to thine own self be true."

Career in the Context of People

Ben never would have guessed his mother's focus on caring about people would become a valuable asset. How does it become the heart of his effectiveness as a leader of various industrial organizations?

By Mr. Ben Benjamin

I grew up in Trinidad, the southernmost island in the Caribbean, in a family that taught me to think about and care for other people. But I had no idea how much this simple lesson of concern for others would become rooted in me through a friend's tragedy and then guide me throughout my career in telecommunications.

As a teen, I encouraged my three close friends to take responsibility for their futures, and we supported each other's successes along the way. I was happy to give, not worried about what I could get from them. It meant more to them than I realized. Very early one morning one of the guys came to my house in desperation. His dad had died during the night of a heart attack. His mom had previously died, and he had come to me because in his view I was the only family he had left. In the depth of his loss, I could see that nothing mattered in his life except people to love him. I had been the one person outside his family to care for him unconditionally, and he now needed that more than ever.

This event with my friend, who to this day is still a great friend, was the start of a life-long journey of evaluating all the choices before me in the context of how they would help or hinder me in caring for other people. Ultimately, the empathy I developed turned out to be my greatest asset as I came to the United States to attend college and begin my career.

After receiving my associate's degree, I moved with my wife and two young children to New Jersey. As a technician in the research division of AT&T Bell Laboratories, I was surrounded by brilliant people with doctorate degrees from major universities all around the world. My technical understanding couldn't compare with any of those Ph.D.s. Fortunately, I understood people and appreciated their special skills. Rather than being intimidated by the talented people around me, I found it easy to strike up friendships and learn from them. I focused on doing my best and avoided comparing myself to others. In turn, people were happy to offer me good advice.

Part of the advice was to keep furthering my technical knowledge and education. I was slowly working toward a degree in electrical engineering as well as trying to understand the American culture, how businesses operated and how I might succeed in my job. I adopted the habit of each evening after work quickly reviewing the day's events. I asked myself three questions: What did I do well, what did I do not so well, and what would I do differently as a result? I also read technical papers to better understand the projects that I was on so that I could be of more value to my team. These habits helped me focus on areas that I could control in my career development and gave me a good technical foundation.

It took me six years to earn my degree, which still left me far behind my co-workers in educational achievement. But that didn't seem to matter to many of them. Rather, they encouraged me by recognizing my various contributions to the work programs. During this time, I also received two promotions. The recognition that I could go about my education differently and still be valued by such an accomplished group was a great gift to my development and kept me pushing forward toward my degree. I was given the opportunity to work at the highest levels of creativity with highly skilled people and the best infrastructure. The only thing that didn't suit my teamwork style was the highly competitive environment.

One such "competitor" was a first-level manager with whom I became good friends. He was committed to developing the careers of those who reported to him, but his commitment came with an expectation of "I will help you, and eventually you will pay me back." Unfortunately, one of his employees, who over a relatively short period of time got promoted twice and became my friend's boss, came to his former manager one day and told him he would need to find a new position in product development. My friend's interests and skills were not a good match for the basic and applied research needed to invent new technology.

My friend viewed transferring from the research division as failure and public humiliation. Instead of being rewarded for his earlier development of his boss, my friend felt betrayed by him. That his boss' evaluation was right – that he would flourish better in the product development environment – was never considered.

While he was stunned at the news, I was stunned that he came and confided in me. He was teary-eyed and distraught as he told me of his betrayal, of essentially being fired, of never expecting this news. He told me that I had a great ability to understand people and situations and did not judge people. In my view, I was so far down the organization – I was two ranks below him – that I was virtually powerless to make any changes. Why waste time making judgments when I had no authority to effect change?

I came away from this encounter with two realizations. First, I did not want to be surprised in my career like my friend was. I became my own worst critic as I carefully evaluated my skill and performance. Second, I stopped the common practice of ranking one division (research) over another (product development). How can working in a place that is a better match for a person be considered a failure? As I realized how I had let the corporate culture limit my ideas of success, I was free to consider completely new options: the other 80 percent of the Bell Laboratories organization that developed products and services for customers.

With that insight, I quickly accepted what I already knew: Research was not a compatible choice for me. I didn't have the right skill set. Plus my talent with team building was not being used. People in research were top in their class in graduate school and most wanted to be number one at work as well. We were not a team but a loose confederation of individual contributors, much like a university.

I stepped up my commitment to my career and pursued engineering positions in the development organizations. I soon took a position with the technical staff in the wireless telephone group and immediately flourished in the team environment. Within two years, I received two promotions and became a second-level manager. I was good at developing teams and getting people in the right places so they could maximize the use of their skills and accomplish more than they thought they could. I loved watching their confidence soar as a result of their accomplishments and seeing more opportunities open up for them. In the midst of this success, I humbly remained my own worst critic, not in a condemning way, but to keep me realistic. I still believed that doing my best is all that I can do because there will always be someone better than me, and I continued my habit of daily reviewing what I did and did not do well and how I could change.

In the early 1980s, shortly before AT&T was forced to divest into multiple companies, I was tapped to transfer the manufacturing operations of our mobile handsets and cordless telephones to Asia. I had to identity an Asian partner and set up the organizational structure. I credit my growing up in Trinidad and my focus on people being a high priority in navigating the cross-cultural setting and successfully completing the job.

That success put me on my vice president's radar screen – he promoted me. Without telling me, he decided that I was well suited for executive management and ensured that I got the kind of assignments that would prepare me for that responsibility. He put me in charge of managing the relationships with our manufacturing partners in Asia. I tried to transfer to other roles several times because I didn't like spending so much time away from my family, but he strongly discouraged me from moving to another assignment.

After divestiture, the company faced both cost and reorganization pressures. My vice president took an early retirement, and based on his recommendation I was promoted to his position. By the time the divestiture's ramifications were sorted out, I was reporting to the president of the business unit and was responsible to more than 500 people for their career development. Putting people first helped me get to this position, but it also added to the pressure of my job. Cost pressures forced us to sell the mobile phone unit, and I was greatly concerned about what would happen to my employees. Most went to the new company, but I was not able to join them. It bothered me that I had no control over how the new company would treat them and how long they would keep them employed.

In the ensuing years as the world of cellular communication exploded, I moved to venture companies, did consulting and served as the chief executive for a few small technology companies. In each role, I went back to my basics:

- I put people first – be they customers, employees, suppliers or owners – treating everyone with respect. As a manager, I learned that one of the best ways to care about people was to identify their talents and skills and give them positions in which they can use them. I have promoted, demoted, fired, transferred and changed assignments for people in order to get them into places where they can flourish. I stopped measuring success by a person's promotions or level in the company. Success is about getting people where they can flourish and then feel good about their contributions and accomplishments – and sometimes means transplanting those who want to be king of the organization. Additionally, as people flourish, they do a better job ... which better serves our customers ... which helps the organization grow ... and allows us to better care for employees.

- I focused on doing my best work and didn't compare myself to others. It reduced complications in the work environment and gave me control of the one thing I could control: my own contribution to the organization's success. I found that as I focused on my own improvement, I could trust that my contribution would be valued and rewarded.

Looking back over my years of working, I am very surprised at how many people, in turn, cared about me. From the very start of my career, people pushed me to get more education and my vice president provided opportunities for me to demonstrate my abilities. I owe much of my success to the care that these people provided.

Was my approach always successful? Sadly, I always found a few people in an organization who exploited other people and situations for their own gain. I wish I knew how to block the behavior of such people or, even better, get them to abandon their strategies of using others and adopt a much better path of cooperating with others to get where they want to go.

These people, thankfully, were the exception. Every once in a while I bump into a person who was in my organization. Sometimes one will tell me that I was the best boss they ever had. I am never quite sure to what they are referring, but it warms my heart to know that I encouraged that person. For me, that's what work is all about.

Take This Job and Love It

How would Jay's up-bringing and educational disappointments in India impact his career in the US? Would it take him away from his keen interests and lead him to a second-best vocation?

By Mr. Jay Jayapalan

School admission tests mark the career path for students in India. So it didn't help that I failed every one I took until I was well into my college education. It started in sixth grade when I failed the written language test for two high schools, and it continued through several college admissions. A friend recently asked me what kept me from being discouraged and giving up. "The support I received from my family," I replied. It was not so much what they told me as what they didn't say – "I quit" was not an accepted attitude at my house. So I kept searching for a new educational path when doors were closed, and in the process I learned skills I would later need to navigate around the obstacles I encountered in my career. Dealing with repeated failures also gave me a sincere interest in helping others.

Although my first degree is in Physics, my college admission test scores for extremely limited seats in graduate school prevented me from pursuing physics as a career. Instead, I entered the Indian Institute of Science to study electrical communications engineering and found myself ill-equipped for the rigors of the program. Thanks to the excitement my professors showed for their subject matter and the help of my fellow students, I kept at it. With their encouragement, I began to enjoy learning and working to my potential. The harder I worked, the greater mastery I gained in my classes. Not only did my self-perception improve, but I began to see how reaching my potential would allow me to make greater contributions to society, both professionally and personally.

I arrived in the United States with my new work ethic, a highly competitive bachelor's degree in engineering and acceptance to graduate school at Kansas State University. I practically breezed through to a master's degree in electrical engineering. The mid 1970s were an exciting time for electrical engineering students, with the new development of microprocessors and digital signal processing. I gained a curiosity for knowledge that has carried me through my entire career in communication engineering – which is a necessity in a field where the technology reinvents itself every few years.

Twenty-five years ago we were striving to send data at 2,400 bits per second wirelessly over analog cellular systems. Today we anticipate sending data nearly 50,000 times faster – at a rate of 100 million bits per second – over the air. In such a rapidly evolving field, my work changes from one day to the next and provides me ample opportunities for growth and renewal without having to even consider switching careers or even moving to a different division in the company. It is just plain fun to be paid to learn about amazing new technologies and discovering ways to apply them to create new and useful products and services.

As much joy as I get from the work itself, I get an even greater satisfaction knowing that my work contributes to an industry that has improved the lives of people across the world. When I was growing up in India, people waited three to six months to have a telephone installed in their home. Today, even people in remote regions can have instantaneous contact with friends and family. Parents can check up on children, children can call home to ask Mom how to fix their favorite dish, businesses can get questions answered more quickly, and help can be called in an emergency. Mobile phones, text messaging, Internet networking sites and email are literally at everyone's finger tips keeping us connected.

Wireless products and the associated software that enable reliable communication save lives. The Internet opens up our knowledge of the world. The benefits of broadband wireless access are just being discovered and will further revolutionize many aspects of how we obtain information. These changes are even more profound in developing countries, where, for example, even street vendors in India who sell their goods out of baskets can manage their business with mobile phones. The ability to access vital information can reduce costs and maximize profits for these micro-businesses. I remind myself of these global benefits whenever I hear about criminals abusing the technology for their own gain.

On a smaller scale, my work also involves service to the colleagues I see every day. I learned from my family that I could ask for whatever help I needed and that others could ask me for help. I was surprised that this attitude of service was not naturally present in the workplace. Early in my career a colleague actually told me, "It makes me sick to see how helpful you are to others." It was a strong sentiment that showed itself more subtly over the course of many years.

One area where few managers seemed to put much effort was in writing performance reviews for those they supervised. Managers often seemed more interested in meeting the deadline set by the human resources department than providing accurate and useful feedback for their employees' career development. After I became a manager, one of my peers remarked "If that field is required to be filled in, just tap the space bar and you won't have to fill it in." Since I was required to do them, I wanted to provide useful information for the individual, not just give a ranking that supervisors can use to decide if someone gets laid off or promoted. Once I learned how to give that constructive feedback and people saw my sincerity and care for them, we were able to break through the management-employee barriers within my organization.

Learning to give constructive feedback began with paying attention to people. I could encourage quiet individuals to express their valuable thoughts in meetings; aggressive individuals to work with an attitude of collaboration rather than push for a quick, solitary solution; and diligent individuals to take time to learn new technologies even when the demands on their time were high.

By the late 1990s, I had developed a good understanding of my mutual love for technology and interest in assisting people. In my work world where one was expected to choose one or the other, I was in a unique position. I turned my career toward a mix of technical and management responsibilities and established a highly motivating career as a manager of technologists who understands both the technology needed to successfully complete a project and the importance of focusing on the people doing the work. I am able to use my technical expertise and leadership skills to provide great career opportunities to other technical people. Our team has bucked the tendency to look out for only ourselves as deadlines approach and has developed a practice of sharing our resources with other teams for the collective good of a project.

We carry that team approach forward to customer service. Fortunately, I work in a culture that focuses on diligently solving problems our customers have encountered when using our products. Customers often express appreciation for the attention we give to their problems, and I too am motivated by the tireless resolve that individuals give to solve customer issues.

Much of my understanding of the true meaning of work came to me during the time in the 1990s as I was redefining my role as a manager. The book *Take This Job and Love It*[13] reinforced in me the higher calling of my career. Life involves more than pursuing wealth and creature comforts; I find meaning through serving others. When I made that connection between my work and how it serves others, it rejuvenated me. I became motivated to perform my daily tasks with excellence because these ordinary tasks are all performed in the context of the people I lead.

I have been a creative part of this great and flawed technological revolution since college. Initially I just wanted to fit in, to find my place. When I began in midlife to desire more meaning and purpose from my work, I found that I could connect the dots between who I was and what I did. Working closely with people toward a common good became as important as developing the newest technology. I am proud to be a productive citizen of the global technical community learning from the collective wisdom of those who have gone before me and trying to do my part to ease the pressure and anxieties of today's rapidly changing world of work.

---

[13] Stanley C. Baldwin, *Take This Job and Love It*, (Intervarsity Press, Downers Grove, IL, 1988)

A Powerful Engine of Business – Section VI

Getting Beyond Our Self

My son filmed a series of television shows for a program on the food network documenting a dozen of the best restaurants in the United States. He discovered a common focus among these restaurant owners, a focus that serves as a perfect example of the success that comes when businesses and managers focus first on people. After filming several restaurants, here's what surprised Brian and prompted him to tell me:

None of these owners are focused on building great restaurants. They all are just thoroughly invigorated by celebrating with their patrons. They create the atmosphere, service and food that give their patrons a great experience. As a result, they have a fantastic restaurant. Yet their motivation is not to create a great restaurant; it's to thoroughly enjoy seeing their patrons have a great time.

These restaurant owners are motivated primarily by their patrons' enjoyment. They use their expertise to establish the right physical ambiance, create an outstanding menu, and hire and train their wait staff. Although they have an unwavering commitment to creating outstanding food and great service and are pleased to have a reputation for creating a fantastic restaurant, they would much rather be known for having an establishment where patrons have a fantastic time. These owners' deepest motivation does not stem from a desire for a particular reputation but simply enjoying the patrons celebrating whatever occasion they came to the restaurant to celebrate.

This motivation affects the way the wait staff is trained. Servers are taught to take their cues from patrons to determine how engaged to be with them. Service focuses on enhancing the celebration rather than providing great service. Of course, excellent service is the outcome – not because of what it does for the owner but because of what it does for the customers. The same applies to the food and atmosphere. Each owner enjoyed the compliments they received for their food and service, but their deepest satisfaction came from knowing that their customers were having a great experience. They exemplified the ultimate in customer focus since they were into it for the sake of the customer.

Many other motivations exist for running a restaurant and can lead to success. Some owners are motivated by excellence and strive to provide a fantastic restaurant where the ambience radiates, the food melts in your mouth and the service is impeccable. They "do" for the customers, rather than "be" with them, a difference that seems to separate the great restaurants from the truly outstanding ones. Another motivation is the cook-it-and-they-will-come approach where the owners focus almost exclusively on providing outstanding food. My wife and I have a favorite Chinese restaurant that seems to be in this category. The atmosphere is average, and most servers do not speak English well, but the dim sum is fantastic. We frequent the restaurant often. Another common motivation is the desire for a steady income. The owner cares about food quality and service because it will generate more revenue. The money in the cash register at the end of the day is the best thank you customers can give.

Four motivations for operating a restaurant – celebration of the patrons, focus on excellence, focus on food quality, generation of revenue – results in a different business model and can result in a highly successful business. But only the first is truly patron-focused. The other three focus first on the owner – care about customer "so that" the owner gains what the owner desires.

Characterizations of the different motivations

The following table summarizes the distinguishing characteristics of the different approaches for each of the four different categories of restaurant owners. The table includes the impact each approach has on the experience the patrons have.

The restaurant owners driven by "Patron Experience" represent the purest form of caring about the patron. The owners enjoy what is important to the patron and design every aspect of their restaurant to meet the diners' desires and enhance their diners' celebrations. The owners' style of operating with diners is a "doing with" rather than "doing for". As a result, the owners automatically create an atmosphere that adds to their patrons' experiences and the staff ends up with a different relationship with the customer. The owners' "Point of Reference" is the customers' experience. They have more fun enjoying their customers than enjoying their business reputation.

Characteristics of Restaurants			
Patron Experience	**Be the Best**	**Cook It, They Will Come**	**Give to Get**
Dominant Motivation — Enjoying what patrons came to celebrate	Reveling in excellent food, service and facilities	Enthusiastic about incredible food	Enjoy doing whatever makes money
Atmosphere — Staff excited about what patrons' celebrate	Wonderful food, service and ambiance	Food is the reason for excitement.	Good service and food
Paton Experience — Staff adds to patrons' celebrations	Patrons celebrate by themselves	It's all about food	Good food and service
Who Joins Whom — Staff enhances the patrons' experience	Patrons join owner in his/her excellent establishment	Patrons join owner in outstanding food	Patrons join owner in his/her business
Point of Reference — Patron experience (**Patron-** focused)	Renowned Restaurant (**Owner-** focused)	Renowned food (**Owner-** focused)	Creation of revenue (**Owner-** focused)
Quality of Experience — Outstanding	Great	Very good	Better than most

In the other three approaches, the "Point of Reference" is the owner and not the patrons, a subtle but important difference that distinguishes the "Patron Experience" from all the others. These other three operate with "so that" thinking. In "Be the Best" the staff focuses on excellence *so that* the restaurant achieves a great reputation; the "Cook It They Will Come" concentrates on providing a great menu *so that* diners are impressed with their meal; while the "Give to Get" treats customers well *so that* they return to the restaurant. The three care about their customers "so that" they (1) gain accolades for being a great restaurant, (2) gain accolades for their great food or (3) establish a financially successful restaurant, respectively. In each case, the owners focus on what the staff delivers and how well they deliver it *so that* they gain what they desire.

These four approaches for operating a restaurant create very different businesses, each successful but only one – the "Patron Experience" approach – moves the focus from the self to something much bigger than our self. This vantage point offers the best chance of being wildly successful. I would hope we could all discover and develop the corresponding vantage point in our industry.

The people who operate the world class restaurants do not fall into the trap of being self-absorbed - desiring to have the best establishments. Their deep-seated desire to enjoy their customers having a terrific celebration propels them to create the best ambiance, prepare fantastic menus, provide wonderful service, and establish effective promotion and advertizing programs, all within the limits of financial reality. These restaurateurs' singular focus on enjoying the patrons keeps them from being self-seeking about having a world-class restaurant. By moving past being self-centered to being caught up in something much bigger than themselves, they end up getting what many people in their profession personally desire – operating one of the world's best restaurants.

An Engine of Business Is Galvanizing Love

What term best describes the owners of the nation's greatest restaurants who are motivated by enjoying the patrons? What word best describes the lube business owner who is motivated to help the employees make the next career step? What characteristic best describes the attorney who is motivated to bring structure to a client's dream? And what term best describes the telecommunications people who are motivated to advance technology for the customers' benefit? As incredible or sappy as it sounds, these businesspeople are all characterized by showing love to their customers. It's not the stomach twitters or hot chemistry that Hollywood defines as love. It's a love that meets another's needs without any thought of gaining something in return. All of these businesspeople actually have gained quite a bit in return, but success was a result of their motive, not the motive itself.

I want to suggest that love is one of the most powerful forces we can bring to bear to ensure business success. Fundamentally, to say that business is all about people is to say that business is all about loving people – customers, employees, suppliers and investors. What is hard to fathom in today's culture of fierce competition where business behavior is most often characterized with war metaphors is that the purpose of business is love. That statement only makes sense with the proper definition of love, one that emphasizes caring about people by doing what is right by people. Dallas Willard's definition of love lays a solid foundation for our discussion:

> "Love is the will [my will] to good or 'bene-volence.' We love something or someone when we promote its good for its own sake."

After we get past the romantic aspect of love, we usually think love consists primarily of compassion, tenderness and empathy. Put in a business setting, a person conjures up the image of a naive person who is too weak to step up to the harsh confrontations, conflicts and clashes of the competitive business environment. Any thinking person instantly knows that kind of love would never have the muscle to be a force in the business world. So we instinctively reject love as one of the powers fueling business and look for other propellants. We rarely, if ever, realize that love amplifies the resources we have for success. Nor do we seek an expanded view of love that provides critical tools for success.

I think it is essential for business success to embrace the full-bodied, robust and comprehensive definition of love stated above, one that contains the necessary energy to galvanize people to effective action that propels the business. In the following pages, I will explain this meaty view of love by applying it to a number of business situations and show that it contains plenty of muscle to do the job. Love is certainly not the only attribute needed to navigate through these situations. Managers also need competency, knowledge and expertise. Yet love needs to be the driving force behind the skills. My list is far from exhaustive, but I hope it is comprehensive enough so you can respond to people with love in the situations you experience at your job. I will give examples of:

- Annual performance reviews
- Stretching a person
- Flying air cover
- Consequences for decisions
- Public correction
- Firing a person
- Creating opportunity
- Market share
- Clear definition of responsibilities
- Inspection of work
- Protection during divorce or serious accident/illness
- Seeking win-win agreements
- Proposals with requests and promises
- Love as Distinct from Duty or Responsibility

Annual performance reviews

Providing a comprehensive and thoughtful performance review that points out the accomplishments of the past year, enumerates a person's key talents and skills, suggests some ways to compensate for weaknesses, sets goals and targets for the tasks of the next year, and establishes some areas of personal development is a great way to love an employee. People want specific examples of how they are contributing. Giving them the particulars is a way to demonstrate love to them. So is an honest discussion of weaknesses and how to compensate for them or to fence them in. Many employees are reluctant to develop new skills, and some are downright resistive. But a manager's push that helps them succeed is love.

When a manager does a performance review because of a sincere desire to help employees excel in their jobs and develop career skills, employees feel loved. If a manager delivers a thorough performance review out of only duty and responsibility, the review is often beneficial, but the employee usually does not feel cared about. When a manager does not do an annual performance review or does it quickly and with little thought, the employee feels disregarded and disrespected.

How employees hear their review will depend on how their manager treats them on a regular basis with his public purpose. If a manager just uses employees to get the job done and gives little thought to what is good for them, the employees will not consider a performance review as valid and useful. They will have a hard time determining what is instructive feedback and what is manipulation and exploitation. Usually the two are mixed together, and the confusion caused by this mixed message is not love.

As I've mentioned before, the skills and experiences we have at work affect us long after we leave for the day. One of the by-products of a performance review is the credibility it gives employees at home with their children. Parents get a report card just like their children. Their work gets graded, and they can talk about their work world with the children using examples from their review. Thus, employees get to use their work experiences to help develop their own children.

Stretching a person

When we send our children to school, we know that we are developing their capabilities by demanding they do tasks they would not volunteer to do. We are stretching our children and helping them become who they can be. When we develop employees, we often force them to do things they do not wish to do. Sometimes their resistance is because they know that when they attempt something for the first time it will not be done well. But I agree with the saying that **anything worth doing is worth doing poorly in the beginning**. Thus, we can help people learn to make effective presentations by forcing them to give their first talk to their department rather than a potential set of customers. Employees forced to do something to increase their competency usually view the experience as painful, not loving, but the discomfort goes away as they master the skill and become effective and confident. Though painful, it is love.

103

Another way to stretch employees is to recognize their innate talents and skills, see how well they are being used and look for opportunities to help them develop more fully into who they could be. If your department does not have the needs to make use of a person's talents and skills, it might be appropriate to recommend the person move to a different division in the company or to another company. That hard decision loves the person.

Employees have an easier time growing when their manager is looking out for them. Few of us, however, have completely pure motives. Even if a manager does not have the best interests of the employees at heart but still forces them to grow, they are actually being loved.

Flying air cover

All of us will make mistakes on the job. It is all a natural part of the learning process. Management has the responsibility to ensure the mistakes made by employees are limited to those that do not cause the failure of the business. When an employee does make a mistake, it usually takes the manager to help the person recover from it. Not only does the manager become the path of recovery, but often the manager takes the hit for the employee when dealing with the consequences to those outside the organization. The manager flies air cover to protect the employee from taking the hit so that the employee can learn and grow. That is love.

The manager often has to hold a meeting, discuss what happened, determine how it can be avoided the next time and define what needs to be done differently. The boss also needs to encourage the person to charge into the next task with enthusiasm. Of course, the person might not charge but limp along. That will strain the relationship between the two. Yet the overall message the employees receives is his manager cares.

Managers also need to fly air cover when defenseless employees are asked to do the impossible. For example, an executive or other manager may place requirements or tasks on the organization without providing the necessary resources or time to get the task done. The manager has to respond to upper management and propose alternatives or make clear explanations of why the request cannot be fulfilled. Such defense of an employee or group is a form of love.

Consequences for decisions

Flying air cover does not mean that we prevent consequences to employees. One of the best ways for developing people is to allow them to experience the consequences of their decisions. When they make a great decision and follow through on it, employees gain the pride of a job well done. When they make a bad choice, they can correct it or make restitution as best they can. In the process they regain the respect of their peers and burn the lesson they learned into their brain forever. It is not a matter of if an employee will make mistakes but what mistakes the employee will make. When allowed to experience the consequences of their mistakes, people are apt to experience a great deal of learning. One of the most loving acts a manager does is to provide the boundaries within which an employee can make mistakes and learn from them. Even though a manager cannot prevent all mistakes, it is critical to limit the scope of mistakes so they are not catastrophic for the company. Employees gaining the pride of a job well done and learning from mistakes are love.

As mentioned in the previous section, the manager often takes the hit for the employee's mistake to protect his or her reputation outside the group. Taking group responsibility for the mistake loves the employee.

Public correction

The manager should not embarrass a direct report in public. However, contentious issues can and should be vigorously debated within the manager's group. But in meetings or situations outside the group, the manager should be careful to not unduly correct a direct report. It is incumbent on the manager to be sure that key priorities and decisions are established before going public. To establish group priorities or mandates by correcting an employee in a public forum is not love.

Firing a person

It is not healthy for employees to continually fail on the job. If attempts to remediate the situation do not correct their performance or employees refuse to accept the evaluation of their performance level, then a manager has no choice but to fire them. A manager cannot care about people and let them continually fail. The loving thing might be to fire them, even if they go to another company and continue the same pattern of failure. The manager exhibits love for both the employee and the rest of the people in the group by refusing to let the person fail in the group.

Creating opportunities

When successful companies create new products and services for customers, management often requires new organizations to implement them. Large, healthy companies almost always have job openings available. People-focused managers don't cling to their good employees. They point their people to opportunities that would be good for them and the company by supporting employees who are pursuing new positions on their own initiative. The manager may require employees to help transfer their responsibilities to others before they transfer. Creating opportunities for employees to seize is a form of love.

Market share

Growing a company creates opportunities for employees. Johnson & Johnson acknowledges this economic reality in the fifth priority of its credo:

> Our fifth and last responsibility is to our stockholders.
> Business must make a sound profit.
> Reserves must be created, research must be carried on,
> Adventurous programs developed, and mistakes paid for.
> Adverse times must be provided for, adequate taxes paid, new machines purchased,
> New plants built, new products launched, and new sales plans developed.
> We must experiment with new ideas.

The executives at GE trumpet market share as a key factor for a successful company. GE is internationally known for focusing on being number one or two in market share in all the businesses in which GE participates. Being well aware of the laws of economics, the executives know that market share drives both the revenue stream and the profit margin. They also know that all employees in many companies are dying a death of a thousand cuts because their company does not command a top position in the market.

GE's resolve on market share leads them to relentlessly sell off divisions that are not able to obtain first and second positions in their respective markets and invest in divisions that have the potential to become major market share entities. As a result, GE's employees have rarely experienced the discouragement of committing to building something that could not be built. This pursuit of market share and the job stability and opportunities it brings is a form of love.

Even though GE is a highly successful company that has gone through numerous transformations, many former GE employees and business pundits object to the manner in which employees were treated in the divisions that were not able gain major market share in the late 1900s. Employees gave the chairman, Jack Welch, the nickname "Neutron Jack".

John Hannah was president of Michigan State University for more than 25 years during the mid-1900s. He caused amazing growth in educational "market share." Hannah brought Michigan Agriculture College from an agriculture school into the ranks of a tier one research university. His leadership transformed Michigan Agriculture College into Michigan State University by:

- Building the country's largest dormitory system and then using it to provide innovative resident education programs
- Leveraging the college of education and hotel and restaurant management program into the leading programs in the world
- Masterfully leading the political process of joining the Big Ten athletic conference
- Consistently out-dueling the University of Michigan for appropriations from the state legislature
- Adding a medical school and a law school to the university
- Being one of the first universities to actively recruit national merit scholarship winners and attract a disproportionate number of them
- Being one of the first universities to have a major focus on international educational cooperative programs.[14]

In the process of growing "market share", Hannah provided opportunities for faculty, staff and students and was universally admired. The press in Michigan wrote glowing stories about him. The staff eagerly propelled the great changes he initiated. Hannah was not known as Neutron John but was revered for his leadership. When he was asked at a private meeting why the next few presidents who followed him were so ineffective, he replied, **"First of all, they don't like people."** Hannah

---

[14] John A. Hannah, *A Memoir*, (Michigan State University Press, East Lansing, MI, 1980).

concluded that the prerequisite for an effective leader is loving people enough to commit to doing what is necessary for their well being, even initiating massive change that they might not initially see as beneficial to themselves or others. He earned their trust and gained their support and as a result, Hannah galvanized thousands of people into action.

Leaders who relentlessly adhere to the financial realities of market share love people.

Clear definition of responsibilities

Management is responsible for dividing up the group's tasks into a sequence of smaller tasks and assigning them to the members of the group. Part of this divide-and-conquer activity is making sure that all members of the group know what their respective responsibilities are and the criteria by which they will know they have successfully completed them. Often it is helpful to understand how these individual tasks depend on each other for success. People usually benefit from understanding how their work adds to overall group and company priorities. Clearly defining the responsibilities and expectations for an individual loves that person.

Inspecting work

We get what we inspect, not what we expect. When we have regular reviews of a person's progress and plans, we are inspecting how the person is meeting his or her responsibilities. When this "inspection" is done correctly, several benefits accrue to the individual. The person gets to establish his or her priorities and be sure they are correct. The person can request any necessary resources and actions needed from the manager to ensure the person's success. The person gets to own his or her responsibilities so they are not micro-managed. Finally, the manager can invigorate the person by joining with the person in what he or she has to do because the manager can make specific and applicable encouraging comments or take action to facilitate the person's next steps. Inspecting a person's progress and plans in order to enhance the person's ability to do excellent work loves the person.

Most of management training provides a comprehensive set of techniques for delegating and tracking the responsibility of an employee. These techniques can be applied in ways that make the person feel either judged, manipulated and discouraged or supported and invigorated. Done correctly, inspecting a person's work loves the person.

Protecting an employee

All of us have witnessed the setback a severe illness, major injury, divorce or other loss has on a person. Any one of these situations will hamper work performance, draining a person of the emotional or physical energy he or she needs to do an acceptable job, let alone an excellent job. The situation can endure for many months and can lead to a public perception that the afflicted person is a marginal performer. This perception might remain long after that person recovers and gets back to being an exceptional employee. In such situations, the perceptive manager can choose to love by "hiding" a person's performance from view while he or she is recovering.

For example, the manager might deem it appropriate to get the entire group together, explain the situation and ask for volunteers to sign up to take on some of the person's tasks. With understanding, the manager can remind everyone that no one is exempt from a severe health or life issue and that the team would cover for them should they ever need it. Further, the manager can shield the person from giving public presentations and being involved in interdepartmental tasks until recovery is completed. Some organizations even allow healthy employees to transfer their sick days or vacations days to another employee when a catastrophe occurs. Protecting an employee while he or she recovers from a big blow loves that person.

Seeking win-win agreements

There are many ways to approach business negotiations and ordinary meetings at work where decisions must be made. Numerous books are written solely on negotiation techniques. Stephen Covey's book *The Seven Habits of Highly Effective People* has an excellent discussion of this topic.[15] The bottom line for me is that treating a person as a teammate rather than an adversary when seeking an agreement ends up loving the other person. That doesn't mean that you avoid all conflict with a customer, employee, supplier or investor in order to get an agreement. It does mean that you go in with an attitude of finding the win-win agreement that all parties can adopt. This attitude usually leads to a more amicable path and better solution that stands a much greater chance of holding up over time. Entering discussions with the assumption that a win-win agreement can be found loves the person.

---

[15] Stephen R. Covey, *The Seven Habits of Highly Effective People*, (New York City: Simon and Schuster, 1989), Part III, Habit 4, pp. 204-234.

Proposals with requests and promises

All the previous examples discuss ways that managers can develop their direct reports. But the support can flow the other way as well. In many jobs, employees are asked to plan how they will accomplish their assignments. One terrific way they can love their boss is to present detailed proposals that request the resources they need and make promises for deadlines for what will be delivered. The boss then knows what is happening and knows who is responsible for what. Informing the boss in clear, concise presentations cares about the boss. The employee benefits as well because the boss might supply resources or take actions that facilitate the employee's effectiveness in accomplishing the work. This is especially true when cooperation is needed from another group over which the employee has no authority. In addition, the boss can sometimes inform the employee that certain deliverables are not necessary or can be scaled back. Accelerating the employee's work and preventing him or her from doing unnecessary work and, thereby, wasting the employee's time is love.

Love as Distinct from Duty or Responsibility

In the restaurant example in the previous chapter, we discussed the different purposes owners had for running their business. The owners who enjoyed celebrating with patrons ended up creating world-renowned establishments. They were not motivated by duty and responsibility but by pleasure – celebrating with their patrons invigorated them.

A commitment to excellence falls one step short of enjoying excellence. Doing a thorough performance review for an employee out of a responsibility to serve that employee (duty) is less powerful than doing it with enjoyment and celebrating his or her growth and accomplishments. Both bring benefit, but employees will respond much more favorably when they sense their growth is celebrated rather than just documented. Communicating enjoyment of someone affirms him or her much more than communicating your willingness to be responsible or do your duty for that person.

I would guess that the restaurant owners who are passionate about patron enjoyment do not find pleasure in every task they perform. But with pleasure driving them, they are able to perform even their mundane responsibilities with a greater energy and higher sense of purpose. Let's apply this idea to parenting. What parents are invigorated when they have to pass out consequences to their children for a bad decision they made? I never was. But as I focused on the character that would be developed in the child as a result of the consequence, I was able to carry through with my actions with a greater sense of certainty and a different kind of pleasure. I was never delighted to have to enforce negative consequences to my children, but I was delighted that I could help them develop into responsible, high initiative, and caring people. Oftentimes, commitment to doing our duty leads to an understanding of its larger impact and we come to eventually enjoy doing it. When we get to that point, we are making a deeper impact in the lives of others. Our work becomes galvanizing love.

I'm not suggesting that a person motivated by enjoyment of others must be outwardly exuberant. Some personalities just do not have that temperament. Usually people on the receiving end of such love understand if a person is not endowed with an outwardly expressive capacity. A reserved personality does not diminish the impact of love when it is given out of a sense of genuine enjoyment rather than duty. No matter what type of personality, learning to live out of a place of celebration is not a trivial task. It takes a great deal of work to genuinely feel that way.

What Love is Not

To understand the galvanizing love I'm describing, it is equally instructive to talk about what this full-bodied love is not. Here are a few examples.

So That – "So that" love is caring about others *so that* they will do what we need or want. Our primary motivation is not the other person but ourselves. We care about employees *so that* they finish the tasks we want done. In our restaurant examples, some owners cared about treating customers well *so that* they would return and the owners would gain the reputation they desired. That's not love; it's manipulation.

It's quite natural to fall into this trap of "so that" love, but being aware will help us climb out sooner. The words themselves provide a great test for determining whether we are caring about people or using them. When I ask someone to do something, can I finish my request with a self-centered "so that"? If so, I'm being manipulative and probably creating anger and resentment in the other person.

Recognizing this self-seeking approach is the first step to recasting our interactions. If something has to be done that no one wants to do, we can approach the need from a broader context: Someone must do it if we want to continue to have a business in which to grow and learn. Perhaps it's a certain group member's turn to do this drudgery. Sometimes a resistance to doing certain tasks indicates an unrealistic understanding of business reality or a substandard performance issue we need to address.

Contracting – A contract indicates I have an agreement or promise with someone. If that person does what I need, I will pay the person the agreed-upon payment. While there is nothing wrong with contracting with another person, we must be careful not to mistake it for love. Contracting is negotiating to a mutually beneficial transaction and has less power and impact than enjoying what benefits the other person.

Networking – A network comprises a set of colleagues who maintain a connection because they may be "useful" to each other in the future. Networking is beneficial, but it is not love. It is mutual assistance and not as powerful as a true friendship. Networking relationships only last as long as both parties see a potential benefit for themselves. Friendship, on the other hand, seeks the best for the other person with no thought to whether our friend is of use to us. Of course, good friends help each other all the time and no one wants to be a useless friend, but the basis of the friendship is not "what's in it for me?" Besides, we still have friends long after the "common interest" dies off and the corresponding network evaporates.

All of these three forms of relating to others – so that, contracting and networking – can provide benefits to people, but none gets to the core of full-blown, galvanizing love: they don't seek what is best for the individual independent of any benefit I might receive. When these three forms of relating are placed within the context of love, the remarkable shift in motivation ignites a giant boost in the power to impact people and, consequently, business success.

For example, instead of networking with people for mutual benefit, we can develop a mindset in which we work to make a colleague as successful as possible without concern for our own gain. Instead of having a network of people who can benefit us, we have a list of people we want to help reach their goals, and we take action for them when possible and appropriate. Of course, if we have a need ourselves, we ask one of them for help – but not with expectation or by laying on guilt. They have the freedom to simply refuse our request.

When It Is Hard to Love

The love I am describing demands a great deal of initiative towards and response to others. To realize how much opportunity we have to love, we can run a simple test. The test involves using the antithesis of love – withdrawal and aggression. A simple check of our reactions and behaviors during a typical day gives us a gauge of how often we either withdraw from people or have aggressive thoughts towards them. What if we added frustration with other people over their actions or inaction? Each of these responses reflects a shortage of love in our fuel tank.

Our ability to love will be put to the ultimate test if someone in the organization becomes malicious and vindictive toward us. That person might inflict pain by blaming us for things we did not do or lying about what we did or said. The individual might even sabotaging our work by erasing computer files or ordering people to discontinue working on tasks that are necessary for our success. Upper management often ignores such situations because it doesn't like dealing with conflict, or it deals with the situation but doesn't think it's appropriate to tell us how. In either situation, it is very difficult to seek the best for the person doing us in. We are much more likely to want revenge, often thinly disguised as a desire for justice, than to want to love that person.

Sometimes love is our first response to someone, but we have trouble sustaining it. Here's a possible scenario: An employee's bad decision has negative consequences for others in the company. The manager responds in love, first, by standing tall and taking management responsibility for the negative consequences and, second, by dealing with the restitution required of the employee. The employee, however, does not own up to what he did. Instead, he blames others and responds with vigorous anger at his supervisor. Now the supervisor is being asked to have enough love to shoulder the blame for her employee's action, absorb his anger and continue interacting with him as he makes appropriate restitution. At some stage of their interactions, the supervisor is likely to lash out at the resentful employee in frustration or deliver a moralizing lecture that does little good. We all know it is not unusual to have multiple situations like this occurring simultaneously. We need a full fuel tank of love to sustain our actions.

Summary

Love being incompatible with business is not the problem; our full comprehension of love is the problem. Our understanding is too feeble, too distorted and too passive to fully equip us to be effective business leaders. Love asks us to look out for the best interest of others, not our own advancement. Love is expressed through our actions, some of which make the recipient feel good while others can be unsettling or stir up anger. Love often calls us to create opportunities for people to grow. It also calls us to face up to conflict.

Love flows more easily when our work is a good match for who we are as people, when we are invigorated by living out our responsibilities rather than operating solely out of a sense of obligation. It's okay to be dutiful – we'll probably get a lot done – but it's even better to enjoy our responsibilities while living out our love. We'll be much more inspiring to those around us if we can move from the smaller world of duty and responsibility to the larger world of love. This is the galvanizing love that dramatically drives business. This is true whether we are the janitor or the CEO.

The framework, "work is all about people", inevitably leads to the engine of business that fuels workers at all levels of an organization. This context for our work is the solid foundation for very healthy ways of interacting with people on the job. Thus, the framework is deserving of our trust and does bolster our career. We can count on it over the long haul.

Flying Air Cover for the Sales Force

Jerry decided to protect his organization from a boss who made a misinformed decision that would damage the company. Would it cost him his job?

By Mr. Jerry Minifie

As the vice president of sales for a large worker's compensation insurance company, I was forced to make tough decisions. The toughest came when I stood firmly for my sales team against a change announced by our new executive vice president and knew I was likely to lose my job.

I was one of about 30 experienced insurance professionals who had joined a well-funded effort to start a new worker's compensation company in our region some 12 years earlier. We had achieved considerable success during those years, and I had risen from the sales ranks to my position as the head of sales.

As I gained increased responsibility, I became progressively aware that I had to a have a clearly defined basis for making decisions as I would have to stand by them when they were misunderstood and even attacked. I felt it would be an important step for me to write down the principles to which I would be committed in my personal and corporate life. At the time, I was very impressed with the idea that a comprehensive understanding of love has a powerful impact on the way we live our lives and the impact we can have. Using this view of love as an overall guide, I wrote the following: "The fulfillment of life consists not in the achievement of things or position or status or length of days; rather, fulfillment comes in meeting life's experiences with integrity, courage, gentleness, compassion, endurance and, above all, love."

I certainly would not pretend that I always followed those principles, but those words sat on my desk as a constant reminder of who I was committed to be personally and professionally. As pressures inevitably came my way, they were a touchstone to keep me focused on the things that really mattered.

A few years later, our highly respected founding president retired and a new president was brought in who did not have a strong insurance background but was clearly well connected in the business community. This was a great asset, as medium- and large-sized employers were our primary customers. The new president felt he needed someone he had a strong history with to help direct our ongoing sales efforts, so within his first year he created a senior vice president of sales position. He hired a longtime friend who had considerable experience as an independent insurance agent. I began to report to him rather than directly to the president.

In a short period of time, my new boss proposed that I make a structural change in our sales staff. He wanted me to reduce the territory and responsibilities of all our regional vice presidents and then take over one of the territories. As I viewed the change, I saw no purpose or value for the company other than to make him look stronger. It seemed to me to be a step backwards for all of the sales people who had been the most significant producers over the prior 12 years.

These people had strong, long-term relationships with key employers (our most valuable customers) in their regions, and I saw no benefit in upsetting the high level of trust that had been established between our company and the employer base we served. I also felt the change would send a clear message to our key sales staff that we did not highly value their role as front-line intermediaries with our most important customers. It seemed clear to me that the sales staff would perceive the change as an almost certain reduction in their income and that some of our best people would likely opt to leave our company.

At the same time, I felt a clear responsibility to the president and the senior vice president to support the directions they felt would be most beneficial to our customers, our employees and our overall company goals. I should say at this point that I was keenly aware that someone my age (late 50s) was not in the most convenient time of life to start looking for a new career.

After further consideration, however, I told the president and senior vice president that I fully understood they had the authority to direct and oversee the sales operation as they saw fit, but that I personally could not make the changes they were requesting of me. They spent the better part of a day trying to convince me their plan was a good idea, but I could not see how this change would benefit the company, our customers or our own people directly affected by it.

The senior vice president said that he would like to have me on board, but if that wasn't possible, he would hire someone else. The president, fortunately for me, said that I was more valuable to the company than the new structure. In the end, we did not implement the plan.

The significance of the experience for me was my willingness to stand firmly for what I believed was right despite the likelihood of severe consequences. I did not consider myself an oracle of wisdom; rather, I felt I needed to act on my own sense of right and wrong and let the chips fall where they may. I'm thankful for the favorable way they fell, but I'm even more thankful for the courage to swing my axe for what I believed in.

Firing a Person Is Loving

Is firing a person loving that person? Katy would discover if that is true or not.

By Ms. Katy Crane

I learned about the working world every night at the dinner table of my Portland, Oregon, home. My father was the owner of a concrete products company, the first one west of the Mississippi River, and he recounted each day's events for my mother, two younger sisters and me. We heard about his meetings with the union bosses, conflicts he resolved and what happened when the Teamsters went on strike. I loved his passion for hard work, his gregarious nature and his thankful attitude. I wanted to be just like him. I just didn't realize that it would take many years before I was mature enough to handle the responsibilities I would be given.

I attended Lewis & Clark College in Oregon during the Vietnam War. We talked inside and outside of class about why the United States had gone to Vietnam and how quickly we could get out. Amid my generation's collective search for meaning, I decided to major in psychology. I also fell in love. Doug and I got married after graduation and moved to Arizona so he could attend graduate school. I found a job working on campus for the dean of graduate studies.

One of my responsibilities was to make collection calls to graduate students who hadn't paid their tuition. The dean was astounded at my success, and I was amazed that he found this unusual. I was just doing what my dad would do. I'd had many conversations with him about being diligent to collect money from people who owed you for the work or product you'd provided. He'd say, "They owe you the money fair and square. Don't be hesitant about asking for it."

When Doug finished graduate school, it was my turn for a second degree. I enrolled in nursing school and after graduating worked with the drive I had seen in my dad. I fought to keep patients alive at the Oregon Burn Center, I gave birth to our two boys, and I changed jobs to work in a doctor's office that specialized in treating diabetes, advancing from a staff nurse to a lead nurse to the manager of the diabetes treatment center.

My marriage did not contain that same passion. Doug had started his own media business, and the demanding work consumed him. I was critical and outspoken about my displeasure. Our marriage began to suffer, and in time we separated. It shook me to my very core and forced me to evaluate all the choices in my life.

In my search for something that made sense, I began to read my Bible. One day as I sat on my couch and read about Jesus, the proverbial light bulb came on and I realized that Doug might never come home but that God would take care of me. It was an epiphany that gave me the strength to stand for our marriage while learning to relinquish all the expectations of Doug that I had developed. Rather than trying to make our relationship work, I needed to let go of what I thought our relationship should be and simply love Doug. Recognizing that at that point he didn't want to hear anything I had to say about anything, I did not contact him – I had to love him from a distance.

We lived apart for a year before we were able to each admit our failings and start over. As I followed the principles of Jesus, I discovered a new desire and capacity to love Doug, which in turn gave me a new perspective in my business career. Not only had our marriage suffered, but Doug was struggling to handle all the challenges of owning a company and managing creative people. He needed help, so I quit my nursing job to join his company. Although we had agreed that we would work together, I was having a hard time seeing how the media business made as positive an impact in people's lives as nursing did. I had to switch my understanding and find contentment and meaning from knowing it was important to support Doug.

Eventually, the work itself also became meaningful. About a year after joining the company I became manager of the products division that created training programs to help companies comply with new Occupational Safety and Health Administration (OSHA) requirements. As a registered nurse at the Oregon Burn Center, I had helped people *recover* from work injuries, and now I would be helping people *prevent* work injuries. I found a deep passion to do much more than produce a training program that would meet OSHA criteria; I wanted to address the deeper issues of why people were getting injured and killed on the job.

In time we separated the companies. Doug continued to run the media business, and I ran the safety training business. I had become a business owner like my dad. Unfortunately, my experiences weren't the adventures I remembered from my dad's long-ago stories. In particular, I had a very difficult personnel decision facing me. We had hired a friend to lead and grow the training business but had come to realize he would not accomplish our expectation. I needed to fire him. Could I resolve this issue with as much dignity as my father would?

I met with our friend and delivered the harsh decision. I told him that we didn't think he was right for the job and that he deserved to work in a place where he could succeed, not one where he was failing. It was a hard conversation, but the right decision if we wanted our business to grow. He disagreed and left the company feeling betrayed and rejected. Eventually we saw that it was also the right decision for our friend, who is now thriving as a business consultant in the Balkan States. He is again our friend, but we had no way of ensuring that when we made the decision to fire him.

That dismissal decision was the first of several I have had to make over the years. The next time was in my role as chairman of the board of a non-profit mentoring organization. The organization was not running well, but I couldn't determine what was wrong. After polling all the mentors, staff members and board members to find the cause of the problems, I learned that the issues centered on the management style of the executive director. She had created an environment of intimidation, and people were feeling beaten down. The board asked me to terminate her employment. Like the friend I had fired, the executive director was shocked and angry but eventually found a position running a small non-profit that was a much better match for her skills.

I was asked to resign as chairman of the board and become the interim executive director. I had a team of six people reporting directly to me, and I soon noticed that one of them – the program manager for the at-risk children we served – was a bad fit for his position. Despite his formal training, he wasn't interested in spending time with the children. Although it was painful, I once again was charged with terminating an employee. I explained to the program manager that he had great qualifications and that he would surely be successful in a new career. He was not ready to give up his salary and risk something new, but I did not relent. I knew he was not right for this position. I later heard that he started a counseling practice and was enjoying his work.

My time with the organization began and ended with the need to terminate an employee. Firing someone is one of the most difficult tasks

I have ever had to do. What helped me through it was realizing the mismatch between the person's interests and skill set and the requirements of the job. Ultimately, a fired employee will be happier once they find a position that better suits them. Thanks to my dad and his lessons at the kitchen table, I now understand that, if done correctly, firing an employee can demonstrate a deep caring for the person, even though it never feels like it at the time.

Passing on a Love for Work

Kent always loved working and being invigorated by it. But he did not know why he loved working. Initially, he was not aware he needed a better "why". Lack of success got his attention.

By Mr. Kent Hotaling

I got my first paying job when I was seven years old working summers in the farm fields around our house. I loved the money I earned. I loved the affirmation I received for being productive. I loved being a worker. As I got older, I felt the personal empowerment that money provided. I had more money than most of my friends to buy the things I wanted and was even able to pay for my college education at a private school. I made plans to study law, which would bring me wealth and prestige. But my well-laid plans didn't go as planned.

While a student at Willamette University in the late 1950s, I met students who helped me begin a faith journey. As a history major, I had a basic understanding of the major world religions and was most familiar with Christianity. Although I knew that it accomplished good things, I couldn't ignore all the pain and suffering inflicted on others in the name of Christ. My friends challenged me to separate Jesus from the religion established in his name by imperfect followers. As I became acquainted with Jesus, his life, the central message of love that he lived and taught, and his invitation for me to become his follower, I found a new purpose for my life. I became convinced that if others could discover Jesus, unencumbered by the religious trappings that had been added, they too would discover a deeper meaning to their lives.

Being a lawyer no longer fit this new purpose. I joined a team of people working with young people and encouraging them to investigate who Jesus could be for them. We set up our own non-profit organization to facilitate our efforts. Thanks to my willingness to learn from my mistakes, I'm still at it more than 50 years later. Our message remains the same – following Jesus sets a solid lifetime foundation on which to build our marriages, families, friendships, values and careers – but our focus had to broaden to address the real-world questions that students, businesspeople, professionals and politicians were asking.

123

Despite my earlier aversion to organized religion, I didn't see that in our early years we were developing some of the same mentality and practices. We planned programs that needed volunteers and funding, and I became focused on the success of those programs. My relationships centered on asking people to join me in my various activities and affirming them for their contributions of money or service to make my programs move forward. I had yet to learn how to be a true friend to people and support them in *their* daily work.

The failure of some of my programs helped turn me around. As I sought to understand what went wrong, I began to see that these programs often kept God at a distance or let people whittle God into a manageable size. He was both much bigger and much more intimate than the programs I had been promoting so vigorously. People wanted to understand how faith could be lived out in their everyday world of work and family. I stopped asking people to come to my meetings and began to meet them where they were – students at their schools, members of the Canadian Parliament at their government offices in Ottawa, inmates in federal prison and business people at their work. I gradually began to see why the ordinary work lives of the people I walked with were so important.

For years I had been telling people the importance of loving others, yet I had never understood that by faithfully performing the responsibilities of their jobs, they were doing just that. I saw that through their jobs, these men and women in government, business and education loved people. The benefits their work brought to people were, to me, God's love made visible. Daily completing tasks as competently as possible provided purpose for going to work each day. The more I can help people see their work and life in this larger context, the easier it is for them to discover their own meaning and purpose at work. They see that their particular skill set is part of something much bigger. With this bigger picture in mind, they are more likely to become invigorated by what they produce or how they contribute at their work or avocation. They don't need to believe the mistaken notion that their work keeps them from God's bigger work of love and restoration.

When my perspective changed, I could see what I had missed for years. A friend in New England, for example, directs the research department for the school system in his community. He daily cares for those in his office, develops creative ways to help teachers become excellent in their work, serves as a sounding board for the superintendent and works hard to improve the education of students in his district. Jesus is alive for him in his workplace, not just someone he worships on Sunday mornings.

Workers asking questions about the connection between faith and work often feel they are traveling alone. My work has involved getting like-minded people connected, either people in the same workplace or those from throughout the community. One such group has been meeting weekly for several years in Kampala, Uganda. Together, these few men and women they have helped government and business leaders gain a broader understanding of the purpose of their work and have provided education and job training for at least 2,000 young people in Uganda.

A member of another group, which included people as varied as taxi drivers, military personnel, athletes and community developers, wrote about the impact the group had on him: "These people were all about propelling people into the world. They were not about creating an organization, institution or movement, but simply about encouraging each other to be and do – *be* who their innate talents allow them to be and *do* whatever it was they deemed appropriate to do. ... They were very effective in their careers and lives because of integrating marriage, family, friends and work into a coherent and synergistic whole rather than allowing their lives to be broken into the typical competing segments. ... They looked at all they did at work as loving people, following Jesus' radical and comprehensive view of love. It became the framework for integrating my career with the rest of my life."

Admittedly, I risk losing a lot of readers when I talk about work expressing love. But I find that this concept resonates with more people than it repels. We have an innate need to receive and express love in all areas of our lives, including our work life. I'm not suggesting we populate the workplace with weak, ineffective, spineless people. I want people to adopt a more expansive, comprehensive and action-packed view of what love actually looks like. If we are to be propelled by caring about people and impacting society in a very positive manner with the goods and services we produce in our work, we have to move way beyond being nice and ratchet up significantly to love in all our activities.

This idea is not strictly a religious point of view. Michael Novak notes that one of the virtues of business is building community.[16] Business

---

[16] Michael Novak, *Business as a Calling*, Work and the Examined Life, (The Free Press, Simon and Schuster, Inc., New York, NY), 1996, pp. 125-128

builds community in order to care about its customers, employees and suppliers. He notes community derives from love in action when he writes, "The economic and the ethical point of a business corporation is to serve others" – customers, employees, suppliers, and investors. Serving is love in action, especially when we finally get to the point where we just enjoy doing it and are energized by doing it.

I have committed many years of travel and work to helping people understand such service, such love. In the process I came to my own understanding: As much as I love to work – as I have my whole life – I now see that love is the work.

Three Tools of the Trade: Competency, Character and Caring – Section VII

A Fully Equipped Player - The 3 C's

Business and industry meet the basic needs of people through the delivery of their products and services. Even greedy, self-centered or marginally competent owners and managers meet the needs of their many customers every day. However, I am encouraging business leaders to follow a higher standard and to expand their competency and character at work and to care about the correct priorities. These three Cs – competency, character and caring – greatly increase a business's ability to benefit society. They help it deliver the highest quality goods and services while caring deeply about all the people along the production line: employees and customers as well as suppliers and investors.

In my consulting business, clients hire me because of my competency, character and caring. These attributes position me to operate with vision, trust and inspiration rather than power, control and fear. The following dialogue (although greatly compressed) represents a typical initial conversation I might have with prospective clients in which they learn what they need to know about me before deciding to engage me in a consulting assignment. I'm in Joe's office at Widget Inc. talking with him about some critical expertise the company needs in order to get its new market-leading product developed.

> *Joe: "We need expertise in the protocols for short messaging service for cellular telephones."*
> *Me: "I helped to write the standard for that and was involved in creating the third-generation cellular standards. If the company could get the messaging capability added to their product, would they have the industry-leading product and a great chance for significant sales?"*
> *Joe: "Yes."*
> *I sketch out a couple of first steps.*
> *Me: "Joe, is my supposition right that this would be the best way to get started?"*
> *Joe: "Not quite."*
> *He explains where I am off the mark.*

127

> *Joe:* *"Do you have any conflicts of interest with any other existing clients?"*
> *Me:* *"No."*
> *Joe:* *"I need to be sure that you can deliver what you promise and can handle our proprietary information appropriately."*
> *Me:* *"That is no problem. The best way to know that is to talk with people I have worked with in the past. How many references or former clients would you like to talk to?"*
> *After a brief conversation, I give him a list of names.*
> *Joe:* *"Do you have time available to work on his project?"*
> *Me:* *"I do. Is it OK if I write up a brief statement of work summarizing what we discussed? Could you review it on Thursday to be sure I heard everything correctly, especially the priorities and payoffs to the company?"*
> *Joe:* *"Fine. Let's do it at 2:00."*

This conversation shows how prospective clients evaluate my competency, character and care for their needs. It begins with my competency to meet their need: "I helped to write the standard." If they don't see in me the expertise to solve their problems, they won't want to know more about me. They will look for a different consultant. If I pass the competency test, they then check my character to see if they can trust me to do the job as promised and to keep sensitive information confidential: "How many references would you like?" Once assured that I have no conflicts of interest – part of the character test – I am questioned about my priorities: Will I care about what is important to them rather than just what is important to me? Will I follow their agenda? My answer: "We'll meet to be sure I have the priorities correct."

Competency – tools for making people successful

Competency is essential for solving client problems and delivering value. In many professions, it begins with formal education and requires various forms of additional education throughout a person's career.

During the formal education stage of life, we work on competency almost exclusively. Education converts our basic talents and interests into skills, which will amplify our ability to love others by being productive at work. Many of us can get overwhelmed with the amount or content of our courses. Why can't we just get to work? The more we know about doing our job, the better we can care about others through excellent workmanship. Developing competence through formal schooling, on-the-job training, management training courses, graduate programs and career-related courses is more meaningful when seeing business as society's delivery system. It takes some work to recast the knowledge gained in formal education into this larger context – few educators will teach you from this context. But seeing what we learn from this context helps us grasp the importance of all our knowledge.

I highly recommend that high school students who are headed to college consider going to an undergraduate school that enhances the pathway to outstanding graduate schools in their field. It is much easier to be admitted to a graduate program when other students from the same university have already been admitted to it and have done well. When it comes to graduate schools, I highly recommend that undergraduates wage a campaign to get into the best graduate school possible for their chosen field. Go to where the best people are. Similarly, when they begin their careers, I would recommend that they wage a campaign to be hired by the best institution in their fields. My first job at AT&T Bell Laboratories provided a base of experience, wide technical exposure and a set of dedicated colleagues that I could not have obtained elsewhere. All were critically important for my development, even after I left the company.

Going to a top graduate school in a person's field and joining a leading institution for that profession adds to competency: It encourages a high standard of excellence. (Excellence is different from perfectionism. Excellence means doing what is required at the appropriate level of quality in the work product. Perfectionists do more than is necessary and waste time and energy that could be used for other useful pursuits.) Having a high standard of excellence forced me to further develop my competencies, which are the tools of my trade. They enable me to turn technology into commercially viable products and services that meet customer needs. Those products and services, in turn, bring real value to society. They are expressions of love to customers and clients.

For those high school students who are entering the trades, I recommend you get into the best training program or apprenticeship you can for your trade. Learn from the best in your field. They will encourage you to set a high standard of excellence for your work. Living in mediocrity results in the emptiness of not being proud of what you do, so avoid it by making a great effort to find a way into the best places for starting your trade.

Character – driver of trust

Competency alone will not maximize my ability to produce excellent products and services. I also need character that earns trust. Character, as defined by Dallas Willard, "is that internal, overall structure of the self that is revealed by our long-run patterns of behavior and from which our actions more or less automatically arise. Character reveals what kind of thoughts, feelings and tendencies a person habitually acts from and gives others an idea of how you will act in the future."[17] For me to be effective as a consultant, clients need evidence of my consistent ethical behavior from the past to ensure I can be trusted in future. They need proof that the proprietary business information they tell me will remain confidential even if I end up consulting for a competitor at some point down the road.

My character took solid root when I first joined AT&T Bell Labs and observed the reality of my work environment. I saw men with questionable values being promoted. I was forced to face some hard questions: What rules for living lead to success in the business world? What does true success even look like? For more than a year, my technician and I, working together on our electronic experiments in the laboratory, talked for hundreds of hours about what values we wanted to live by in business. We discussed people we respected, biographies of people with character and where various philosophies would lead us.

I wanted to bet my career on something that would endure an entire lifetime. We defined a set of criteria that allowed us to start with the end in mind and work back to the values and practices that would get us there. The criteria essentially showed our definition of success – making positive impacts on society and people, rather than solely moving up the corporate ladder, and being respected by our wives and children both for who we were and what we did. The set of criteria that our conclusion had to satisfy included:

- Leading with vision, trust and inspiration rather than power, control and fear.
- Creating highly effective teams even with people of diverse and strongly held opinions.
- Attracting the best and most competent people.
- Committing to what is best for the employee.

---

[17] Dallas Willard, *Renovation of the Heart*, pp. 142-3.

- Allowing people to reach their full potential, i.e., propelling us to fully develop and use our innate talents.
- Being trusted by employees.
- Committing to excellence rather than mediocrity.
- Making the hard decisions that are required to produce excellence.
- Being transparent without hidden agendas and schemes.
- Allowing solid friendships to grow out of working together.
- Being the same person at home and work.
- Being a person my wife and children would respect.
- Having no regrets when all is said and done.

Interestingly, over the succeeding months, we slowly but surely eliminated various views of a philosophy of working. Among the top approaches we rejected were the following:

- Resume thinking – aggressively pursuing those types of job assignments based upon what will make a résumé look fantastic.
- Professional reputation – feverishly working to make sure as many people as possible know about our accomplishments and their resulting impact.
- Impress the boss – committing to be the most in tune with what the boss wants, doing all we can to meet those desires and, of course, reminding the boss of what we did.
- Be the difference maker – using all means to maneuver into highly visible positions where we can gain that reputation.
- Paper the world – being first to get the memoranda out to people or having as many journal publications as possible.
- Promotion path – finding out what it takes to get promotions and aggressively pursuing those assignments.
- You scratch my back, I'll scratch yours – creatively stimulating others we depended on to do their part so we can look good to our boss.

We rejected all of the above because they spring from a foundation of self-centeredness. This "all-about-me" outlook failed to meet a number of the work criteria we were trying to live by. It would put us in conflict with our co-workers. It would not lead to teamwork. It would not allow friendships to grow. Each view flunked other criteria as well. It was not hard to see the reason for rejecting them.

The philosophy we chose resulted from the process of elimination. We did not conclude that one way was the best but that all the alternatives were worse. We were not left with an option we excitedly chose but one that seemed way too simple and ordinary: We had to do our ordinary job with excellence – be extra-ordinary – while being committed to the best for co-workers. We broke it down into four parts:

1. We had to take care of our own business, which most often would benefit our co-workers
2. We would commit to make others successful whenever we could
3. We would stay out of office politics and just do what was right as best we could determine
4. We realized from the biographies of the people we respected that we were involved in a marathon and not a sprint.

Many of the people we studied had their greatest success later in life – including former Miami Dolphin head coach Don Shula, who led his team to a perfect season and two Super Bowl titles, and former UCLA basketball coach John Wooden, whose teams won 10 NCAA championships in 12 years – but the foundation for that success was laid much earlier. We needed to take a long-term view when making today's decisions.

It was one of the first conscious decisions I made in inventing my career. I could have benefited greatly from having a much more comprehensive understanding of this view of work. But my friend and I were on our own. At the time, I did not have evidence from the workplace or support from people that the choice I was "left with" would lead to success in my career, but I adopted this view of living at work as best I knew how. After all, what choice did I really have?

The decision I made took hold. I suppose it was because we spent so much time exhaustively understanding and then rejecting the alternatives. I think we kept hoping that one of these rejected options would pan out because the one we were stuck with did not have much appeal. There was no assurance that our choice would bring good results in the long run. I never wavered from or reconsidered my choice during my entire career. Decades later my career did reap the benefits of this fortuitous choice.

In the short run, however, my value system did not always lead to desired results. In fact, my character got me fired for exactly the same reason I now get hired – I would not compromise my integrity. I was working for a company whose sales were declining rapidly because new technology had made the products obsolete. The president wanted me to deceive those who worked for me into thinking the company was doing financially better than it was. I refused to lie for him and was asked to find another job. Eventually my colleagues found out why I left the company and are now my best character references for potential consulting clients. Character choices led me to take a stand that cost me my job. That same character now gets me hired. Who would have thought that what seemed so awful at the time would end up being so valuable?

Caring – committing to the right priorities

Very few people work in total isolation. Most often we end up collaborating with others, whether co-workers or customers. Deciding whether we will care only for our own interests or also for theirs greatly affects the impact of our work.

What we care about will either make a clearing in which others can operate or leave no room for anyone but ourselves. A serendipitous interaction I had with a client illustrates this concept. In my consulting, I make a point of being part of my client's team. Usually I am charged with importing new technology into a technology-driven company and have to work hard to get people to buy in and own the new technology. The best way to do that is to be seen not as a consultant but as a member of the team, just as committed to the project's success as everyone else. During one such project, I was walking down the hall with the company's CEO when he suddenly blurted:

> **Tom:** *"You really are a consultant, aren't you?"*
> **Me:** *"Of course, I am. What did you think I was?"*
> **Tom:** *"I have hired numerous consultants over the last 30 years, and you are the first one that did not have an agenda other than consulting. Everyone else did consulting as a means to doing something else, like starting their own company or getting a job. But you just want to be a consultant and help others succeed."*

Later I learned that the CEO had been searching for my hidden agenda for months and could not find it. The CEO eventually saw that I was motivated by a simple desire to meet customers' needs, which would contribute to the company's success. Simply wanting the client's company to succeed breeds trust, undergirds teamwork and propels

133

communications. Of course, simply enjoying the company's success expresses a form of love.

Caring about my client's success makes me more effective than other consultants who are viewed as people doing a service only to make money. The CEO saw that I was genuinely excited about his company's success and had a strong motivation to meet customers' needs, which ultimately contributes to the company's success. My strategic involvement also enabled the employees to enjoy their work more. I had not realized that my enjoyment of the company's success as my root motivation was so unusual and effective.

If we are motivated primarily by a desire to get credit for our contribution, we inherently create competition between ourselves and everyone else. We are no longer a team player. People get very annoyed if we constantly point out our key contributions to a project or if we take complete credit for a collaborative effort. It might be tempting in competitive environments – such as top-tier research universities that demand the highest professional reputations for their staff – to steal credit that rightly belongs to others. If we do, however, we eventually will lose valued team members. Who wants to work with a person who has to hog all the credit?

The only people likely to join the team of a person operating with a "what's in it for me" philosophy are others out to get something for themselves. This self-centered dynamic will not foster healthy teamwork or, ultimately, customer satisfaction. I once worked for a large corporation ($6 billion a year in sales) in which one of the top three vice presidents was passed over for a CEO slot at a subsidiary. He subsequently left the company. I asked the existing CEO why this highly competent person who made major contributions was not selected. He said the person was primarily focused on what he personally got out of his career and did not have the best interests of the company and its employees as his primary focus. Had this vice president become a CEO, his self-serving values would have engendered a culture of self-centeredness for the entire subsidiary.

If we're honest with ourselves, most of us are like this vice president at some point in our careers. In the first half of my career, as I was exploring why my industry and my role in it were important to society, I attempted to obtain meaning from work. I relied on others to see and appreciate the contributions I made. I expected them to affirm me for the excellent work I did. I expected them to thank me for my commitment and attitude. Moreover, I relied on this recognition to motivate me to continue my excellent work. I rarely got the feedback I craved, and my energy waned. The usual work hassles further drained me.

Once I realized my industry and my role in it were important to society, my motivation came from the intrinsic value of my career itself and I engaged in it with great energy. I was invigorated more by my deep and engrained purpose for working than by positive feedback from others. Even the hassles and the tedious details of any job had a way of invigorating me. However, I still do enjoy the recognition from my peers when it occurs.

Sometimes the word "drive" is used to describe what we care about. We all are driven by something. Drive exposes the internal ambitions that motivate us. Either we will care about others and make room for their concerns and needs or else we will care only about ourselves and compete against others. We either will help others gain energy or will drain their fuel tanks. We either will help others catch a noble vision or fuel their resentment at being used and abused. Ultimately, we can help build a team that mutually invigorates each other or a team that antagonizes each other.

Summary

It is much easier to follow a leader who knows what to do (competency), is trustworthy (character) and provides a vision (caring). Warren Bennis, the noted professor of management at the University of Southern California, summarizes the three C's when he says,

> *"An effective leader balances these forces [competency, character and caring]. Drive [caring] without competence and integrity [character] produces a demagogue. Competence without integrity and drive manifests a technocrat. Someone who has ambition and competence but is void of integrity is a destructive achiever. We've seen all too many of them."*[18]

Developing competency, character and caring gives us powerful ways to love people. They are the tools we use to meet people's needs and create organizations that function effectively. When we persist long enough at using these love muscles, we enjoy a deep feeling of significance for

---

[18] Anita Thompson, "A Look at Leadership," Costco Connection, March 2004, pp. 16-18.

being part of the delivery system that serves society's well being. Our work matters when we value something much bigger than ourselves: the welfare of other people – our customers, employees, suppliers and investors.

Having the perspective that work is all about people is absolutely congruent with the tools of the trade. With the combination of the two, we become fully engaged in our work. Entrusting our career to this framework provides coherence with essential personal attributes that allow us to complete our deliverables with excellence.

From Wealth to Riches

Mark's commitment to become wealthy stimulated the development of his competency and character even though he initially committed to a goal that was inappropriate for him. Chasing a goal towards disaster ended up bring good fortune.

By Mr. Mark Thomas

I was born to be an entrepreneur. As a young teen delivering the daily newspaper in the quiet morning darkness, my imagination raced. Every day I saw myself as the owner of a new business, one that earned me a lot of money. I wrote down all my dreams and ideas and shared them with my grandmother, a retired Chicago real estate broker. She encouraged me to develop my thoughts and be even more creative. My passions had awakened and she kept fanning the flame.

By high school I was translating my hopes into reality. Fueled just as much by my parents' confidence in me as my grandmother's support, I started a tractor painting business that employed several of my friends. I also formed a flagpole construction company. Driven by my passion for self-employment, I began to create a plan for a business in the world of personal finance. In the 1970s, long before the financial planning industry was born, I understood the need to offer my clients service and value. In return, I would be wealthy and respected.

I established financial goals with age-specific benchmarks. I would be a millionaire by age 30 and pay taxes on my first million dollars of annual income by age 50. I graduated college with a triple major and mapped out the next five years. I had hoped to be hired after graduation by any of the local stock brokerage firms in Billings, Montana, but I settled for a position selling life insurance, confident that it was a stepping stone, not my life's career. I committed five years to the job so I could develop my understanding of the industry and my communication skills. I also fell in love with a woman who believed in me and shared my appetite for entrepreneurial risk. The daughter of a rancher, Karen knew the importance of integrity and hard work, and she agreed to become my wife.

This manic drive was the result of more than my hard wiring and encouraging family. I also had something to prove. I was a reckless boy diagnosed with dyslexia at a young age. I paid regular visits to the school's speech pathologist. I wore orthodontia strapped around my neck and a football helmet on my head (a precautionary measure prescribed by my family doctor to protect me from further head trauma). I was determined to prove that, despite appearances, I was smart and likable. I assumed leadership positions and worked hard to be a success. Even after my teeth and speech were corrected, however, my self-worth still needed adjusting.

Our first child was born at the beginning of my insurance career. I was devoted to him and Karen, but I could see that the demands of being a good father and husband conflicted with my vow to be a millionaire by age 30. My struggle worked itself out in a dream I had one night as my son lay sleeping in the next room.

I was standing in the checkout line of our grocery store with my shopping cart overflowing with cash, all large denomination bills. My few groceries were in the seat of the cart, where a toddler would sit. As I handed my first purchase to the clerk, she looked at me and described the items: "So you want a fantastic marriage to the bride of your youth." "Yes," I responded. "I expect we'll travel through life until 'death do us part.' The clerk rang up the cost of loving my wife: time away from business opportunities. Her price was high, but I gladly dipped into my cart and counted out the sum. She pulled out the next item: "So you want a life grounded on a foundation of faith." She counted out a large sum of money to pay for it.

I continued buying my items. I purchased the admiration of my children and the respect of my friends and business associates; I bought honesty, integrity and service. Everything that I desired to be or have came with a high price, yet I was willing to pay. As I left the store, my cart had much less money in it, although still enough for my family to live on. In place of the cash, I now possessed the values and priorities that made my life complete.

I was startled by the vividness of the dream and can still see it today, more than 20 years later. It became my defining moment, a reminder of my core values and the bedrock for my decision making. It did not mean that the decisions were easy to live out – I struggled with balancing my roles of husband, father and provider. As I had hoped, I was learning a lot selling life insurance and enjoying the business relationships I was developing and was invigorated when solving clients' problems. But I was not the independent business owner I wanted to be. At times I saw myself as a water boy: anticipating the needs of others, serving them, refreshing them, and working to facilitate their objectives. Could I let myself relax my self-imposed expectations and see the value of the skills I was forming, the relationships I was developing and the lessons I was learning?

I became plagued at times with fear. My commitment to serve others gave way to a fear of rejection. My desire to provide for my family raised fears of financial ruin. My confidence to tackle irritating obstacles crumbled into fears of the humiliation that I would feel if I failed. I battled these fears for years, slowly overcoming them with the help of an older gentleman who became my mentor. When I met Dick Smith I saw a man of moral integrity who I wanted to emulate. This older gentleman gently helped loosen the stronghold fear had on me. Every day I made a conscious decision not to live in fear, but to build a business based on opportunities and caring about clients. Through this process, more business opportunities began to present themselves.

Although Dick focused on the growth of my character, he helped me to see work in a much bigger context that allowed me to relax more and become more creative. He urged me to embrace opportunities and rely on Karen's intuition and insight. He also assured me that a professional career would emerge that would be more exciting and fulfilling as long as I was willing to follow a career path that was sure to lead me to three or four new opportunities over the next 40 years.

As it became painfully obvious that I would not be a millionaire by age 30 and as my five-year insurance career stretched out to 15, I followed his advice. Karen and I shared our financial concerns with each other and began to imagine and clarify our future business. I saw how unrealistic profit expectations of corporate stockholders put increased pressure on a sales force to sell products to an uninformed public. Absent in the financial service industry was an up-front, open relationship with the client. This vacuum in the traditional financial service industry gave birth to the new industry of registered investment advisors who serve as an employee of the client, not a sales machine for a profit-hungry corporation. My interests fit perfectly with the emergence of this industry.

In time Karen and I launched Capstone Wealth Management and became independent financial advisors to clients. I was certainly not at the frontier of fee-based financial consulting, but I introduced the concept to our community. We were developing the business model as we went along, learning step by step what fit our personalities as well as looked out for our clients' financial interests. We did not try to copy another firm or assimilate what brought success to others. We lived with a big dream and little income.

My personality, passion, experiences, values and beliefs became the DNA of my business model and personal life. By working within my abilities, I created a life that invigorates me. My business is difficult, the stakes are high for my clients, the liabilities are great, and the leadership of my employees can weigh heavy at times. I take these responsibilities seriously, yet I am content. One measure of whether a person is working within his gifts is how he notices time. I often lose track of time and the day is gone before I know it. My occupation suits me well.

But it did not make me a millionaire by 30. Instead, at age 48, I measure my wealth by a different standard. As I shifted my focus from earning riches for myself to growing my clients' wealth, I gained riches greater than I could have anticipated. I've built deep, caring relationships with others. I have faced my fears and followed my dreams. Both of my children respect me for how I persevered through my life's difficult times and are able to face their own challenges with confidence. I work hard, run an honest business and serve my clients as best I can. Best of all, I am still in love with the woman that caught my eye in 1981. Karen's confidence and trust in me has proven to be of greater value than any appetite for material pursuits. As self-serving as my original wealth goals were, they set me on the path to claim the true riches of life.

Being Equipped for Starting a Business

Growing up on a working farm with parents that emphasized the formation of character provided Lyn with the inner compass and work ethic necessary to create, build and lead. Swanson's success as an entrepreneur rests on the quality of his 3 C's. But even so, the journey was fraught with persistent challenges.

By Dr. Lyn Swanson, Ph.D.

As a research scientist and technology entrepreneur, I've traveled a long way from the 20-acre California farm where I grew up. My dad's education ended in eighth grade, and few of my 20 or so first cousins who lived nearby went to college. But my childhood offered plenty of fodder to help me decide to major in science and remain in college for four years of undergraduate studies, three years of graduate school and two more of post-doctoral studies.

Perhaps my mother's career in nursing had some impact or the suggestion by a friend studying veterinarian medicine that majoring in a science discipline might lead to a good career. Perhaps I was inspired by the space race triggered when the Russians launched Sputnik and President Kennedy challenged Americans to focus on science and technology and be the first people to land on the moon.

Most likely the biggest influence was my curiosity into how things worked. The farm offered untold treasures for me to take apart...much to my Dad's frustration. How else could I learn how things worked? My curiosity to discover how the spark coil of a Ford Model A operated easily transformed into the curiosity of a graduate student into how molecules were put together and a familiarity with such esoteric topics as statistical thermodynamics, quantum mechanics and atomic physics. Curiosity is vital to scientific research in the physical sciences. Fundamental truths regarding natural processes can be explored and verified by experiment. The basic mechanisms can then be explained within the context of reliable physical and chemical laws and mathematical constructs.

My family had few resources to commit to a college education for me or my two sisters. Miraculously, scholarships covered all of my undergraduate and graduate school expenses. I was able to attend a private liberal arts college thanks to a football scholarship. My two roommates were also on football scholarships and, unlike most of our teammates, one majored in engineering and the other in geology. They provided a supportive environment for me as I chose to major in chemistry. I thought my studies might lead to a medical or pharmaceutical career, but upon graduation I was offered a scholarship to launch a doctoral program in physical chemistry at a major university.

I enjoyed my graduate and post-doctoral studies in basic research in surface and charged particle physics. I would have been content to continue post-doctoral studies indefinitely, but by then I was married and starting a family, and I needed a more permanent, better paying job. I found one in Oregon that allowed me to continue doing research in my same area of interest. As a new dad cut loose from the protective university environment, I began to think more seriously about the impact, if any, my work would have with respect to future career opportunities, my family and society in general. My questioning took my mind back to the farm and all that I learned from my childhood.

My parents' lives exemplified the importance of discipline, honest work and a respect for each other and the land, and they expected us to follow their example. I started working during summer vacation – for 75 cents an hour – at the age of 10. By 12, I was operating a tractor, irrigating, pruning grapes and performing many other necessary jobs on our farm and on a large peach and almond ranch where my Dad and one of my uncles were foremen. These years with my extended family developed important character qualities that I would need as I moved forward in my career choices, qualities such as:

- **Patience** – Whether I was cultivating a pasture, pruning or irrigating an orchard, or hoping for a raise in my hourly work rate (when I worked on our farm it was for room and board), I learned that to enjoy the fruit of my labor required a great deal of patience.

- **Frugality** – Born to parents who lived through the Great Depression of the 1930s and the food and gas rationing of World War II, my sisters and I learned how to have fun in ways that didn't require material possessions. Hunting crop-eating jack rabbits, raising farm animals for a 4-H project and fishing with Dad at the river stand in stark contrast to my grandchildren's iPods, video games and 12-speed bicycles.

- **Dependability** – My dad worked as a ranch foreman until the day he died (much too young at the age of 60). He worked from 7 a.m. to 5 p.m. six days a week with one week of vacation a year. The landowner could depend on him without reservation to run the ranch, and I was thrilled whenever he let me go with him to work and I could see his dedication to work as if the ranch belonged to him.

In 1971 I started FEI Company, an electron microscope business, with two colleagues as a side activity to my main role as a faculty member at an academic institution. Not until 1987 was the business of sufficient size that I was able to resign my faculty position and devote full time to the business. Patience was required.

During the start-up years, the business could not afford to rent space in one of the desired high-tech business parks. An unpretentious, small building at a nearby airport had to suffice. Financing to start the business came from the three founders, all of whom had young families to support and mortgage payments to make. Frugality was required.

The employee count during the first several years of the business was small, and each one had to assume important responsibilities. Because I was working full time as a faculty member at a nearby research and graduate education center, my connection with them was limited. Knowledge that each employee would effectively carry out their responsibilities was essential. Dependability was required.

Interspersed in my research, academic and business life was a four-year period as an academic dean at a liberal arts college. Dependability, patience and wise use of limited resources were as important in managing a college faculty and academic curriculum as they were in my business and as they were for my Dad managing farm workers in the almond and peach orchards in the San Joaquin Valley

By 2002 when I retired as chairman of the board, the electron microscope business that we started in the basement of the physics building in 1971 had grown to 1,800 employees with operations in three countries. Much of the core technology that propelled the growth of FEI came from my early research in academia. But I owe the company's success to the many colleagues, students and employees involved in the enterprise over those 40 years. Each one has been an encouragement and help to me, and I trust the reverse is also true. Although one measure of a company's success is the profit it generates, I give greater value to the positive impact a company has on the lives of its employees and customers. It's not surprising that I value people over money. I learned that lesson years earlier, on the farm.

Conclusion: Pathways to the Hidden Treasure in the Work We Do

Having a correct vantage point for viewing work is incredibly vital when searching for the purpose of the work we do. If we have an inappropriate vantage point, the problem becomes intractable. Have a right one and it's inevitable - the answer emerges. Seeing work as being all about people (customers, employees, colleagues, suppliers and investors) structures the search dramatically. Contrary to our first impression, this framework is not inadequate, implausible and ineffective but stimulating, invigorating and powerful enough to propel a 40 year career. We can have confidence that as we persist, answers will emerge and mushroom into deep-seated motivations.

When we finally discover the hidden treasure in the work we do, we end up engaging in our jobs very differently. We get "caught up" and "lost in" something much bigger than ourselves as Mark Thomas' transformation from riches to wealth illustrates. We no longer see ourselves as simply workers but have a sense of destiny. Michael Fargo ends up with a most unusual, but highly effective, context as an IRS agent with his sense of purpose.

More likely than not, we see ourselves as being in "business for our self" where our present employer is our current client.[19] Even though that view gets us to see ourselves in a context larger than our present organization, our commitment to the organization becomes greater than it would be otherwise. We live in the strange paradox where we commit more to the organization's objectives but care less about its success. The context Darvin Avis adopts actually transitions him into his own industrial machinery repair business while Gwen Barrett creates a very unique marriage and family environment.

The discovery of purpose seems to come in as many different forms as there are people. For some, the moment of discovery is sudden. Bill Simmons has a startling revelation about the contribution of the people

---

[19] Rabbi Daniel Lapin, "Don't be a 'Wage Slave' – Be in Business for Yourself", *Thou Shall Prosper*, Second Edition, (Wiley & Sons, Hoboken, NJ), 2010, pp. 74-77.

in his MasterLube business. Dick Sawdey latches on to an off-hand comment of a client appreciation for structuring a dream. For others, the awareness grows gradually. Katy Crane (moving people out of failure), Diane Doherty (small business development), Serena Morones (power of accounting) and Charlie Glendinning (advocating for educators), all have such experiences.

All the narrators graphically portray that the journey rarely follows a straight line. The pathways to the hidden treasure in our work have unexpected disappointments, undesired surprises, and numerous dead-ends. Michael Fargo (IRS agent), John Gilman (pastor and pilot) and Michelle DeYoung (integrated life) simply persisted and kept looking for answers from the larger context. At some point on the long and lonely journey, people recognize the importance of what they do. From that point forward, they bring meaning to work rather than attempting to get meaning from work. Their 'vocations' come to life as they use their creativity in unique ways to meet the challenges.

Some lead to unexpected places as Jay Jayapalan ends up in a technical career after all, Ben Benjamin ends up in executive roles he never expected and Lyn Swanson ends up running a company rather than being a professor. While Jerry Minifie made a decision that put his job at risk. Others, like Kent Hotaling, ended up staying in a single career but see their involvement in a much richer and larger context. On the other hand, Mark Thomas stayed in the same industry but ended up leading his own financial firm.

But they are all ordinary people who be became **extra-ordinary** simply by being "excellent at the ordinary aspects of their jobs". They all have a deep sense of satisfaction in what they do. None have wide notoriety; most have little or none. They all have a great sense that their lives have significance by seeing their work in a larger context than they originally did. The vantage point they knowingly or unknowingly adopt ends up being the key. They stayed with that vantage point long enough to uncover their purpose.

Most narrators embrace their insignificance in the much larger picture from which they view their work. Paradoxically, the realization of our insignificance in the larger picture gives us our real significance. Each views his or her contribution from an expansive vantage point; allowing each one to see the hidden value of their work more clearly. In this larger context, they more readily discover the importance of their industry to society and their critical role in their organization even though they know they are replaceable.

They experience liberation from the discouraging world of meaninglessness to full engagement in a world of purpose. Their views transform their perspective and motivate them to be caught up in something much larger than themselves. Not one dwells on material success but they all celebrate those rich moments when they discover real purpose in their lives. Not one has a hint of regret or sense that they wasted large portions of their lives, even though they passed through experiences they certainly would not want to repeat.

The stories reveal people are the central focus, including customers and employees. The storytellers hone their competency, strengthen their character and clarify what they care about, and in the process increase their effectiveness with people. As their purpose for work gains clarity and their ability to articulate it gains precision, the atmosphere of their work place changes. The purpose they communicate about the meaning of work is infectious. Other people begin to catch bits and pieces and they engage, initiate and respond accordingly. In short, others piggyback on the person's purpose and enjoy work more, too.

All of the people make a difference right where they work. They unleash unique creativity by faithfully persisting over sustained periods of time in their careers and avocations. They gain a sense of personal destiny that powers them through the mundane tasks in their jobs. Most create a unique working style that impacts a wide array of people with very little extra effort simply by seeing their work in the bigger context. They become more satisfied and less self-absorbed by getting lost in their purpose for working. These people realize that:

- The vast majority of the products and services resulting from our work end up caring about people in concrete, specific ways.
- While we produce the products and services, we also get to care about the people with whom we work in terms they appreciate.
- As we work to bring out the best in others and ensure their success, we strengthen the links in our interdependent business world and deliver better products and services.
- Being "extra-ordinary" - doing our ordinary tasks with excellence - produces extraordinary results.

- Being "extra-ordinary" over a sustained period of many years leads to a tremendous sense of personal satisfaction and significance.
- All these actions encompass a full-bodied love that unleashes a powerful force for good in society.
- By seeing the purpose of their work in the bigger picture, their creativity flourishes and leads to meaningful impact.
- Finding the unique purpose for the work we do may take a couple of decades or more.
- The journey to discovering our purpose usually has dead ends pursued, inappropriate goals chased, and unfounded expectations demolished.

Each person demonstrates that when the larger context of work is all about people - customers, employees, suppliers, and investors – successful outcomes result. Moreover, a comprehensive understanding of this perspective embraces all of the realities of the work place and provides congruent answers to many of the dilemmas we all encounter. They find their perspective compatible with successful companies and highly effective people. The numerous successful businesses and people that have gone before us leave a trail of convincing evidence this framework leads to meaningful pursuits. The vantage point can be trusted; we can put our weight down on it with confidence; it is bedrock. All the individual stories illustrate that if we root our work in this context, we end up with a very satisfying career. Not a single story ends with the individual holding an empty bag filled saddled with regrets.

Our careers, occupations and avocations – where many of us spend the majority of our days – allow us to join with others in delivering products and services of incredible value. Seeing our contributions from the larger vantage point shows our work matters. Businesses, government, education, non-profits and avocations – our work – help us meet each other's needs and gain the dignity that comes from contributing to the good of society. Our work holds a great hidden treasure of purpose we each get to discover. We each get to join the adventure of encouraging others to experience their own unique story. Let's just **GO FOR IT**!

Acknowledgements

I am grateful to the numerous people whose participation made this book a reality:

The Storytellers

I am very appreciative of all the individuals who took the time to distill their thoughts and write them down. These real-life stories of people who relentlessly persisted through the confusion and uncertainty of their own scareers make the concepts of this book come alive. For a few of them, I have had the distinct pleasure of having a front-row seat during their entire career and have learned much through their persistence and where it took them. Our friendships have deepened during our long journeys together.

My Family

Orleen, my wife, has traveled with me since 1966 and has been a co-inventor of my career. She stood by even when it was not clear we were on the right path. Her insights cleared the fog many a time when I was trying to discover "what is wrong with this picture." All three of our children and their wonderful spouses have helped bring order to the jumbled explanations of many of my concepts and topics. I have been encouraged through our numerous family discussions on these topics.

My son, Brian, requested stories to illustrate the concepts. He remembers **stories** better than abstract ideas. My son-in-law, Jake, wanted me to detail the discovery and invention process to show **how** concepts were discovered, not just **what** was discovered. He knows he has to discover and invent for himself. My son-in-law, Jason, requested material on how to get in position to discover and follow your career. He is committed to being on the playing field and wants ideas on **how to** not waste his efforts. My daughters Joan and Julie and daughter-in-law, Catherine, have each asked some penetrating questions that made me think more deeply. Clearly, all are also keen inventors of their own careers and avocations.

My Friends and Colleagues

I am indebted to many terrific colleagues who encouraged me – sometimes nudging and sometimes shoving – during various points in my working life. Some of these people have their stories included in this book. I am also deeply grateful to the board of advisors of my consulting business. This group has cared enough about me to push me very hard to increase the scope of my business. That push initiated the string of events that resulted in this book. They see both opportunities and skill sets that I completely undervalue. This group has been a wonderful gift for over two decades.

John Gilman and Kent Hotaling

Kent Hotaling and his colleagues set Orleen and me on this journey of integrating marriage, family, friends and career into a coherent and synergistic whole. Nearly 40 years ago, they gave us the framework within which to see all of life. It has served us incredible well. What a ride we have had!

Kent and John Gilman approached me to join them in writing a booklet on this same topic. The reaction to the booklet stimulated this effort. Many of the people who related their stories in this book have been long-time friends of Kent and his wife Kay. Kent slogged through many revisions with me as well. Thank you both for spending so many months writing and rewriting.

My Editors

Lee Lueck labored valiantly to help convey the message. Her clear thinking and command of the English language improved the clarity in a remarkable manner. I am greatly impressed by her talent and skill. My sister, Sue Baugh, a published author and editor, provided invaluable advice for navigating the publishing business. Without such advice, I doubt you would be reading this book.

Rick Baugh
work@crbaugh.com

Appendix – The People and Their Stories

Here are brief sketches of the people who told their stories. Each followed a different path to discovering why they do what they do and why it matters. Together, their backgrounds create a rich mosaic of the incredible diversity of meaning we can bring to our work. We all get to be a part of this much larger picture, of which these stories are but a mere hint.

- **Darvin Avis** has spent nearly 40 years in the trades, starting out as an auto mechanic and ending up running his own one-stop industrial machinery and boiler repair company. He loves the challenge of keeping all kinds of machines humming away.
- **Gwen Barrett,** as a full-time homemaker in Salem, Oregon, created a place of hospitality and support for her husband, children, and adopted family and local, national and international guests.
- **Ben Benjamin** came from Trinidad to the United States to attend college and spent more than three decades at AT&T Lucent. He started out as a laboratory technician and ended up eight promotions later as a vice president. He subsequently has been CEO of other high-tech companies.
- **Katy Crane** spent four years as an intensive care nurse in a burn unit before joining her husband in his corporate communications business and then founding her own corporate training company. She also has served as executive director and board member of a non-profit organization that mentors at-risk youth.
- **Michelle DeYoung** is Managing Director of an Australian-based management consultant firm that specializes in creating high-performing work organizations through business re-engineering and facilitating cooperative partnerships between employers and employees. She has lived and worked on four continents.
- **Dianne Doherty's** first career was raising four daughters. After the relentless part of that career was over, she returned to college and started her own public relations firm. She now helps small business owners propel themselves toward successful operations.
- **Michael Fargo** started working at age 13 and spent the next 18 years working in at least 14 different fields on three continents. He eventually settled down and spent the next 29 years working for the IRS.

- **John Gilman** earned his living as a pilot but has also spent his entire adult life helping people discover purpose in their lives and develop a clear picture of who Jesus is.
- **Charlie Glendinning** studied graphic arts in college and hated it. Then he discovered a love for the art buried within the confines of graphics through hard labor at a print shop. Today he is the art director of the American Federation of Teachers.
- **Kent Hotaling** has journeyed with hundreds of people as they've discovered who they are and invented a life that fit their interests, passions and talents. Even after 45 years, he's excited to see people set their life on a solid foundation and charge into society.
- **Jay Jayapalan** came to the United States from India to earn his master's degree in electrical engineering. He spent his career designing products for the telecommunications industry.
- **Jerry Minifie** spent more than 40 years in a variety of people-oriented positions including ministry and sales. In the final 15 years of his career as an insurance executive, his major focus was investing in people.
- **Serena Morones** is a CPA with her own firm in Portland, Oregon. She and her husband have worked with the needy people in Rwanda for the past 10 years.
- **Dick Sawdey** spent his entire 40-year career dealing with legal matters, first as a lawyer and eventually as a vice president of a large publishing company. He started his own firm to help people order their legal affairs and help realize their dreams.
- **Bill Simmons** moved from selling cars to servicing them. For nearly three decades, he has owned and operated a highly successful oil and lube business, where he invests in launching his employees into their long-term careers.
- **Lyn Swanson** left the California farm where he grew up to become a scientist, engineer, professor and entrepreneur. He recently retired as chairman of an electron and ion-beam microscope company he and two other friends started 30 years earlier.
- **Mark Thomas** spent the first 15 years of his career selling insurance and learning the skills he would need to launch his own business. He then seized an opportunity to establish a client-focused financial planning firm.

Biography - C. R. (Rick) Baugh, Ph.D.

In 1991 Rick founded his consulting firm. He has been a part-time Chief Scientist for several small and medium sized telecommunications companies. He also has been part of the initial team for several telecommunications startup firms. In the last ten years, Rick initiated a thrust for individuals to "invent their career". Dozens of people elevated their careers to a whole new level of effectiveness. Creating an environment where people see their careers from an entirely different vantage point and then discover the energizing purpose they bring to their work has been extremely satisfying and rewarding.

1970 marked the year that Rick began working at AT&T Bell Laboratories doing fundamental research in the emerging field of digital telecommunications. He then designed and developed business communications products. Leaving Bell Laboratories 11 years later, he took a job as Senior Director of advanced technology at Racal Datacom, a manufacturer of high-speed modems and multiplexers. Subsequently, he headed the engineering organization of a startup telecommunications group at The Boeing Company.

During Rick's career, awards came his way - Fellow of the Institute of Electrical and Electronic Engineers (IEEE) for his contributions to digital communications and the IEEE Centennial Award. His 14 patents and more than 20 professional publications document his technical innovations. He served on advisory boards for several colleges of engineering at major research universities.

Rick is one of the first few individual in the world to receive a Ph.D. in computer science (University of Illinois). His undergraduate years at Michigan State University (Electrical Engineering) were a most enjoyable and formative time.

Rick married his college sweetheart Orleen, and they thoroughly enjoy their three adult children and their terrific spouses as well as their grandchildren.